NORWAY

Sakina Kagda

MARSHALL CAVENDISH
New York • London • Sydney

Reference edition published 1995 by
Marshall Cavendish Corporation
99 White Plains Road
P.O. Box 2001
Tarrytown
New York 10591

© Times Editions Pte Ltd 1995

Originated and designed by
Times Books International, an imprint of
Times Editions Pte Ltd

Printed in Singapore

Library of Congress Cataloging-in-Publication Data:
Kagda, Sakina.
     Norway / Sakina Kagda.
       p. cm.—(Cultures Of The World)
     Includes bibliographical references and index.
     ISBN 0-7614-0181-4 (lib. bdg.)
     1. Norway—Juvenile literature. I. Title. II. Series.
DL409.K34 1995
948.1—dc20   95–14897
                              CIP
                               AC

INTRODUCTION

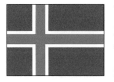

THE NAME NORWAY comes from *Nordweg,* meaning way to the north. Norway is well named, as almost half of it lies north of the Arctic Circle. The North Cape, located on Norway's Magerøya Island, is the northernmost point in Europe. Norway is a land of majestic mountains, breathtaking fjords, and snow-covered plateaus.

Norwegians are a tolerant, independent people who care deeply about issues such as human rights, civil rights, and equality of the sexes. They are also deeply committed to promoting peace and have sent 40,000 of their troops on United Nations (UN) peacekeeping missions. The people have a strong sense of national identity and a desire to retain an independent position at a time when borders and national characteristics are disappearing in Europe. *Cultures of the World Norway* presents Norway's fascinating mix of tradition and modernity.

CONTENTS

Many people have a pre-conceived notion that all Scandinavians are tall and blond.

CONTENTS

Norwegian children find
convenient resting places
at the Vigeland Park of
sculptures.

GEOGRAPHY

NORWAY IS A LONG, narrow country that sits at the top of the European continent. It covers an area of 125,017 square miles (323,878 square kilometers). This number does not include Norway's overseas territories, which include Svalbard, a group of islands in the Arctic Ocean; Jan Mayen, a volcanic island northwest of Norway; and, in the Antarctic, Bouvet Island, Peter I Island, and Dronning Maud Land, which is a large chunk of the Antarctic Coast between longitudes 45°E and 20°W. Nearly two-thirds of mainland Norway is mountainous. The more than 160,000 lakes and as many islands found in this northern country testify to the ancient glaciers that once scoured its land and coastlines with the movements of tremendous masses of ice, earth, and rock.

Opposite: **Norway's population distribution is 26 persons per square mile. As most people gravitate toward the cities, vast tracts of land are as sparsely populated as these fields in central Norway.**

Below: **A trekker surveys the mountains and valley of the Romsdal district in western Norway.**

Early Norwegians relied on fables to explain their country's remarkable land formations. To account for the hole in this mountain on Torghatten Island, legend has it that a horseman shot an arrow at a maiden, but hit the king's hat instead. Today, we know that after the Ice Age, the sea level rose, and erosion by water and frost caused the hole.

MOUNTAINS

Norway is one of the most mountainous countries in Europe. Its mountain ranges extend almost the entire length of the country. The glaciers shaped the peaks into such odd forms that they have provoked the images of trolls and other supernatural spirits. The mountains in the south, which contain the highest peaks in Europe north of the Alps, are called Jotunheimen, or Realm of the Giants.

A few mountains are so steep that no one has ever attempted to scale them. Some have been attempted only in recent years. The 2,000-foot (609-meter) Reka in north Norway has never been climbed. The Troll Wall in Romsdal (western Norway) was first climbed only in 1967. Many consider it the most demanding climb in Europe. The retreating glaciers cut some mountains down into *vidder* ("VI-der"), or mountain plateaus;

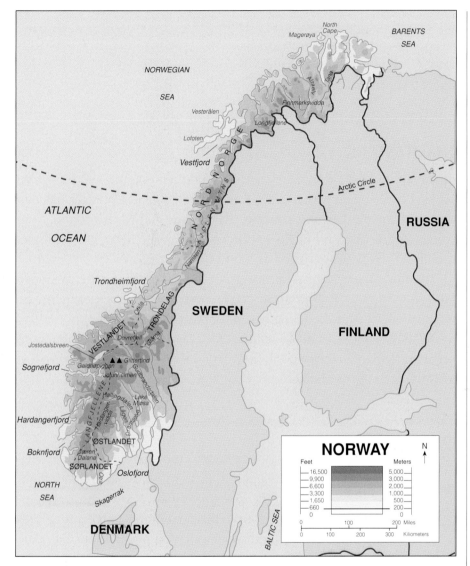

As a mountainous country with a dense river network, Norway produces mainly hydroelectric power. Most of its power stations are hydraulic installations in high mountain regions.

others were ground down by the weight of the ice sheet, one and a quarter miles (two kilometers) thick, into flat plateaus called *fjell* ("fyehl"). The most impressive legacy of the glacial erosion in the uplands are the *fjords* ("fyords") of western Norway. These are very deep and narrow inlets of the sea between steep cliffs. The fjords of Norway are sometimes even deeper than the North Sea, although they are often shallower near the coast, where the ice sheet was thinner.

REGIONS

For centuries, the Norwegians have divided their country into four main regions. Vestlandet (West Country) and Østlandet (East Country) make up the southern third of the country. Trøndelag (Mid-Norway) and Nord Norge (North Norway) make up the rest. Recently, however, Sørlandet (South Country) has emerged as a fifth distinct region.

The three main regions of the south are defined by wide mountain barriers. From the southernmost point, a swelling complex of mountain ranges, collectively called Langfjellene, or Long Mountains, runs northward to divide Østlandet from Vestlandet. An eastward sweep of mountains separates Østlandet in the north from Trøndelag. Where the southern half of Norway ends, northern Norway, or Nord Norge, begins.

A coastal ferry provides transport service to the people living near this fjord in Vestlandet.

VESTLANDET The West Country is the Norway best known to the rest of the world—a Norway of beautiful, well-kept villages and coastal towns nestled against a backdrop of majestic mountains. The ancestors of many Norwegian Americans left from this area in the 19th century. This narrow coastal zone reaches into the Atlantic Ocean and has many islands and steep-walled narrow fjords cutting deep into the interior mountain region. The major exception is the Jæren Dalane (Plain), south of the city of Stavanger, which boasts the highest agricultural yields in Norway due to its rich soils, very mild winters, long growing season, and abundant rainfall.

SØRLANDET Centered on the city of Kristiansand, this southern area has an idyllic coastline that has become Norway's foremost summer vacation area. The land is hilly, but the growing season is slightly longer than around Oslo, Norway's capital. The interior of Sørlandet, with narrow valleys running up into the beginnings of Langfjellene, is very sparsely populated, and the people of the scattered settlements depend on dairy farming, sheep raising, and forestry. Sørlandet is usually considered part of Østlandet.

ØSTLANDET The East Country boasts more than half of Norway's population, most of whom live in and around the metropolis of Oslo and in the region around Oslofjord. Although this area is mostly urban and industrial, there is also agriculture, mostly in the lowlands extending eastward and southward toward the Swedish border. With sufficient rain, the highest summer temperatures in Norway, and rich soil, this land is intensively cultivated. The largest forests in Norway are found between the Swedish border and the Glåma river, east of Oslo. The coastline facing Denmark across the Skagerrak passage, stretching from Oslofjord to the southern tip of Norway, is densely populated and crowded with small towns, villages, and small farms.

The harbor at Risør, one of several towns along the southeastern coast of Norway. Once this harbor was a regular port of call for trading ships. Today it is popular with tourists and artists. Its attractions include well preserved wooden architecture of 1865–1900, the Wooden Boat Festival, and the Chamber Music Festival.

11

About half of Østlandet is forested. The region has a little more than half of Norway's total forest resources and a similar share of the country's total area of fully cultivated land. In mining and manufacturing, Østlandet is also responsible for more than half of the nation's total production value and of its total trade. These large shares of the national wealth, combined with the concentration of economic activity around Oslofjord, secure for Østlandet the highest average income per household in Norway.

TRØNDELAG Mid-Norway, also known as Trøndelag or the Trondheim region, is centered around the long Trondheimfjord. Trondheim, the

Trondheim, a city well situated at Trondheim-fjord, will be celebrating its one thousandth anniversary in 1997.

region's major city, is the third largest in Norway. Trøndelag has less industrial development than Østlandet or Vestlandet because there are fewer good sites for power stations. On the eastern shore of the fjord is a small agricultural area.

NORD NORGE Mountains with jagged peaks and ridges fill most of this region, even on the many islands. A long string of large islands jutting into the Atlantic west of Vestfjord form the Lofoten Wall. Numerous fjords scissor into this narrow strip of Norway's northern tail. Northern Norway has one of the most irregular coastlines in the world, even more irregular than in the southwest. Nord Norge has a frontier quality as an experiment in northern adaptation.

Nord Norge has been called the "the weather kitchen of Europe." Rain, clouds, mist, and fog are characteristic of much of the Norwegian coast, but gales and squalls add a special quality to the north, which has some of the highest recorded wind speeds in the world. Norway's first meteorological station was established there in 1866. As is often said in Nord Norge, there is a lot of weather to watch.

The Norwegian poet Nordahl Grieg (1902–1943) said of Nord Norge in 1922: "This is the real Norway: freezingly sparse and beautiful."

Winter days are longer the farther north one goes in Norway.

CLIMATE

Without the warm waters of the Gulf Stream, which keep the fjords from freezing, Norway's coastal areas would not enjoy temperate and mild climate all year. Even past the North Cape, which is farther north than both Siberia and the continent of North America, there are many green forests and, on sunny days, the beaches are strewn with sunbathers.

Average temperatures for the southern part of Norway near Oslo and Bergen range from freezing in winter to 61°F (16°C) in summer. In northern Norway, the average winter temperature is 23°F (–5°C), and the average summer temperature is about 50°F (10°C), although temperatures have been known to reach as high as 77–86°F (25–30°C).

Norway lies directly in the path of the North Atlantic cyclones, which bring strong winds and frequent changes in weather. Western Norway experiences comparatively cool summers, mild winters, and a substantial amount of rain. Eastern Norway, sheltered by the mountains in the center of the country, experiences warm summers, colds winters, and very little rain.

LAND OF THE MIDNIGHT SUN

The amount of daylight and night varies from one place to another due to the tilt of the Earth's axis and the season of the year. At the equator, there is hardly any noticeable difference between the number of hours of daylight and the number of hours of darkness, and between summer and winter. The farther north or south one goes, however, the greater is this variation. Located as far north as it is, Norway experiences great variations in seasons and in hours of daylight and night.

In the northern half of Norway, the sun does not set all summer. The area from the Arctic Circle to the North Cape is called the Land of the Midnight Sun and attracts thousands of tourists. The length of time the sun stays above the horizon declines as one goes south, but the sun never sets on Midsummer's Day (June 23) in all places north of the Arctic Circle.

Even south of the Arctic Circle, summer nights are so bright that people can read their newspapers by natural light in the middle of the night. It is not unusual for Norwegians to take a walk or visit friends at 2 a.m. Norwegians say they have two days for every summer day: one for work and one for *hverdagslivet* ("vehr-DAHGS-leev-uht") or daily life.

To make up for all that sunlight during summer, in winter those who live north of the Arctic Circle do not see the sun for weeks, although there usually is some brightness around midday.

When the sun reappears in late January, after two months of continual darkness, children in Tromsø in northern Norway get the day off from school to watch its arrival. They have to be prompt to greet the sun, for on that first day it is above the horizon only four minutes.

The Arctic Circle Center is a popular tourist spot. It is situated 1,970 feet (600 meters) above sea level, in the Saltfjellet National Park.

NEW TERRITORIES

In the late 19th century, Fridtjof Nansen's polar expedition came within 272 miles (438 kilometers) of the North Pole. Less than two decades later, Roald Amundsen's expedition was the first to reach the South Pole. Norwegian exploration in polar regions brought new territories under Norway's sovereignty in this century: Svalbard in 1925, Bouvet Island in 1928, Jan Mayen Island in 1929, Peter I Island in 1931, and Dronning Maud Land in 1939.

SVALBARD This archipelago located in the Arctic, 352 miles (567 kilometers) from the northernmost point of mainland Norway, consists of four large islands and a number of small ones covering an area of 39,000 square miles (62,700 square kilometers). The largest of the islands, Spitsbergen, accounts for more than half of the archipelago's total land area. The landscape is characterized by steep mountains and deep fjords, and vast areas are covered by glaciers. Coal is an important mineral resource, and oil and gas are being recovered by mining companies. Svalbard's population of nearly 4,000 people is concentrated at Longyearbyen, Ny-Ålesund, Barentsburg, and Pyramiden.

ANTARCTIC ISLANDS Norway's three territories in the Antarctic are Bouvet Island, Peter I Island, and Dronning Maud Land. Norway was one of 12 countries that signed the Antarctic Treaty in 1959. In 1991, these countries agreed to maintain the Antarctic as a nature reserve devoted to peace, research, and environmental cooperation. Mineral extraction activity in the area is prohibited for 50 years from 1991.

THE LOFOTEN WALL

The Lofoten archipelago is sometimes referred to as the Lofoten Wall, perhaps because its islands form a barrier between the northwestern coast of Norway and the Atlantic Ocean. The total area of the Lofoten islands is 475 square miles (1,230 square kilometers), and the principal islands are Austvågøy, Vestvågøy, and Moskenesøy. The Lofoten islands are famous for their fisheries. Amateur anglers haunt the fishing villages on the islands during the cod season, from January to April. The Norwegian Fishing Village Museum and the Dried Fish Museum are both located at Lofoten.

Reine, on the eastern coast of Moskenesøy, is situated in a calm bay.

MAJOR CITIES

Norway's three major cities are Oslo, the capital and home to about 500,000 people, Bergen, with a population of about 200,000, and Trondheim, which ranks third with 140,000 people.

OSLO Norway's capital, situated at the head of the Oslofjord, is the country's main center for communications, trade, education, research, industry, and transport. It is also Norway's political and financial center, and its center for international shipping. Oslo was founded by King Harald III around 1050, but it became the capital of Norway only in the 14th century. It was destroyed by fire in 1624 and rebuilt as Christiania. Its name was changed back to Oslo in 1924.

BERGEN The natural center of Vestlandet, Bergen has had a more international character than any other city in Norway since the Middle Ages, when it was an active trading center of northern Europe. It was officially founded in 1070 by King Olav III, "The Peaceful" (ruled 1069–1093). Unlike Trondheim and Oslo, Bergen has no fertile land and lies amid seven mountains facing the sea. Said to have been a starting point for many Viking expeditions, Bergen grew as a fishing and trading port. Today, Bergen is the second largest city in Norway and is still the principal port on the west coast, with a considerable merchant fleet, several large shipyards, and one of Norway's four universities.

Dockside houses, seen from a ship in Bergen's harbor. The houses were built by the Hanseatic League, an organization in north Germany and neighboring countries formed to promote commerce. In 1980, these houses were included in UNESCO's World Heritage list.

TRONDHEIM Trondheim, in Trøndelag, is Norway's historic capital. It was founded in 997 by Viking King Olav Tryggvason (ruled 995–1000). In the Middle Ages, Trondheim was an important commercial, administrative, and religious center. Norway's first abbey was built on an island outside the city, and Nidaros Cathedral, an important pilgrimage site, is here.

Trondheim, Norway's technology capital, has been a research center since at least 1760, when Norway's Royal Scientific Society founded a museum and research station in the city. Norway's first seat of learning is a school founded by the Nidaros Cathedral monks. In 1900, the technical school was transformed into a college, known today as the Norwegian Institute of Technology. SINTEF, a state-funded research institute, concentrates on marine and information technology in Norway and abroad. The national Ship Research Institute is located here, as well as a biological research station with an aquarium.

OTHER CITIES Apart from being the oil capital of Norway, Stavanger in southwest Norway is the center of agricultural research. Tromsø, Norway's largest center north of the Arctic Circle, is home to the world's leading research center for Arctic phenomena.

An aerial view of Oslo's waterfront. Oslo's location between mountains and the sea gives its residents many advantages, including skiing in winter and sailing in summer.

The Atlantic puffin's most distinctive feature is its large red, yellow, and gray-blue bill. The depth of the bill enables the bird to catch and hold fish.

Top: A herd of mountain goats on Hardanger Plateau. The area is famous for goat's milk cheese.

FAUNA AND FLORA

Reindeer, wolverines, and other Arctic animals live throughout Norway, although in the south they are found only in mountain areas. Elk are found in the forests and red deer on the west coast. Although common as recently as 100 years ago, now the bear, wolf, wolverine, and lynx are only found in a few areas, mainly in the north. Foxes and otters are common, and badgers and beavers inhabit many areas. The beaver is an example of a successful program of protection. Prior to 1940, the entire European stock of beavers was around 500–600 animals, largely found in southern Norway. Protection increased their number, to the extent that Norway was able to send beavers to Switzerland, Russia, and the Czech Republic.

A small rodent periodically found in large numbers is the lemming. People speak of a lemming year, when mountainous regions teem with thousands of these small animals, providing predators with a rich food source. The dazzlingly white snowy owl of the North Pole flies thousands of miles to a good supply of lemmings. How it knows when lemmings are plentiful is one of nature's mysteries.

Nesting cliffs are filled with millions of kittiwakes, puffins, guillemots, auks, cormorants, and gulls. The sea eagle, an endangered species about four decades ago, is now thriving. Lakes and marshes are inhabited by crane, whooper swan, grebes, geese, ducks, and other waders.

Along the coast, there are large numbers of seals and whales. Most rivers have fish, notably trout and salmon. Large schools of salmon are found in at least 160 rivers; this attracts anglers from all over the world.

Norway has about 2,000 species of plants, but only a few, mainly mountain plants, are particular to Norway. Thick forests of spruce and pine thrive in the broad glacial valleys in eastern Norway and in the Trondheim region. In western Norway, there are virtually no conifers. North of the Arctic Circle, there is little spruce, and pine grows mainly in the inland valleys. The pine, spruce, and other Norwegian conifers, such as the juniper and yew, retain their needle-like leaves throughout the year. In winter, the needles curl up to retain moisture. Wild berries grow throughout Norway, including blueberries, cranberries, and cloudberries, a species that belongs to the rose family and is little known outside Scandinavia and the United Kingdom.

Climate is a prime factor in determining the distribution patterns of plant life in Norway. Along the west coast, the winter is mild and snowfalls rare. Plants that cannot tolerate frost, such as the star hyacinth and purple heather, thrive here. Farther inland grow species that can withstand short periods of frost and snow in the winter: the foxglove and holly are typical plants. Around Oslo, the long, cold winter and dry, warm summer provide the right climate for species like the blue anemone and the aconite.

Norwegians call these blue anemones *blåveis* ("BLOW-vays"). They are one of numerous species of flowers that appear in the wilderness every summer.

HISTORY

THE EARLIEST TRACES of humans in Norway were found along the coast of Finnmark and north of Stadlandet in the west. Archeologists believe these humans lived between 8000 B.C. and 9000 B.C., by which time most of the glacial ice had receded. These earliest inhabitants may have migrated from Finland and Russia around 10,000 B.C., when the interior was still covered with ice. Another theory is that they came considerably later from the south and traveled northward.

THE EARLIEST FARMERS

Before 3000 B.C., the inhabitants of Norway lived in tent-like shelters or coastal mountain caves. They hunted and fished. Between 3000 B.C. and 1500 B.C., warlike Germanic tribes migrated to Norway. From them, the earlier inhabitants learned to attach handles to tools to make them more efficient. It was during this period that eastern Norway was settled by other migrants, farmers who grew barley and kept cows and sheep. The hunter-fishers of the west coast were gradually replaced by farmers, although hunting and fishing remained useful. This gave rise to permanent farming settlements, which were usually situated along the coast and near lakes.

Isolated from each other by mountains and fjords, the farming communities became independent small states with their own leaders. By the A.D. 700s, 30 states existed in Norway. By the 9th century, the states were divided into districts, each with its own assembly, where grievances were settled in accordance with written laws.

Rock carvings in Nord-Trøndelag tell the story of early inhabitants.

Opposite: **An old gateway in historic Bergen.**

The lawmaking assemblies—the Gulating in the west, the Frostating in Trøndelag, and the Eidsvating in the east—came into existence by the year 900.

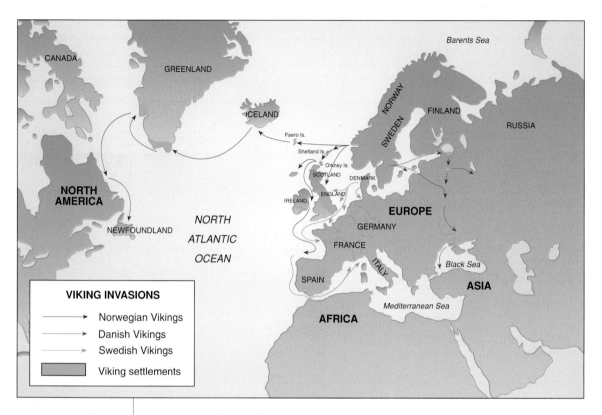

VIKING INVASIONS

→ Norwegian Vikings

→ Danish Vikings

→ Swedish Vikings

▨ Viking settlements

The Swedish Vikings sailed east to Russia and visited Constantinople (Istanbul). The Norwegians and Danes headed west and south toward Europe. The Norwegians primarily headed west, raiding and settling in northern England and Scotland, going south through the Irish Sea to Ireland and down to Wales. Later, they traveled to Iceland, Greenland, and North America.

THE VIKINGS

Perhaps the most famous Scandinavians are the Vikings. In the Viking Age (A.D. 793–1066), the Scandinavians set out over the oceans to conquer new territories and expand their markets. One theory is that the rapid population growth that seems to have occurred from A.D. 600 led to a shortage of land, prompting many to look overseas for their fortunes. The Vikings came from Norway, Sweden, and Denmark, and each had different routes of conquest and trade.

The Vikings were the only Western sailors in early medieval times who dared to sail beyond landmarks into uncharted waters. They discovered Svalbard, the Arctic islands northwest of Norway. Before A.D. 1000, they had settled all the habitable islands in the North Atlantic, including the Shetlands, the Orkneys, Faeroe Islands, Iceland, and Greenland, which all remained under Norwegian influence for centuries. They also landed on the shores of North America 500 years before Christopher Columbus.

VIOLENT VIKINGS The Vikings had a reputation of being pirates because of the warlike raids on other European communities that characterized the first 100 years of the Viking Age. The earliest recorded raid of the Norwegian Vikings was on Lindisfarne in 793. Landing quickly and unexpectedly on the island of Lindisfarne off the northeast coast of England, a small party of raiders looted the monastery, set it on fire, slaughtered many monks, and took others captive. Then they sped away in their dragonhead boats, disappearing as quickly as they had appeared. This left the English in a state of shock, for they had not believed such a sea attack possible. This success encouraged the Norwegian Vikings to launch more raids against northern England, Scotland, and Ireland. Monasteries were the first targets because they had wealth and few defenses. These small pirate raids were then followed by larger, bolder, and better-organized attacks, sometimes with military expeditions of dozens of ships under a commanding chieftain.

Norwegians themselves see the Viking times as more complex. Many claim that not all Norwegians of that time should be called Vikings, only the warriors. They point out that most Norwegians were farmers and fisherfolk, quietly going about their daily lives.

The raid on Lindisfarne was the first recorded Viking attack. Alcuin, an English scholar in Charlemagne's court, described the raid: "Never before has such a terror appeared in Britain as we have now suffered from pagan race, nor was it thought possible that such an inroad from the sea could be made."

This reconstruction of a Viking house shows how the Vikings lived: the house is a single long room with timber walls, a dirt floor, and a roof covered with shingles and grass. Large pieces of stone reinforce the walls. A hole in the roof allows smoke from a hearth to escape. There are no windows, and light enters only through the doorway and slits in the wall, so the room is dark and musty.

CREEKMEN OR WARRIORS?

The origin of the word "Viking" has long been a mystery. Some scholars believe it meant "creekmen," basing this on the Old Norse word *vic*, meaning creek or inlet. Others insist it referred to a pirating center, the Vik, in the Oslofjord. Yet another theory is that the term originated from the Old English word *wic*, meaning warrior.

The Europeans whose lands were invaded by Vikings did not do much speculating on the origin of the term and did not differentiate Swedish Vikings from Danish Vikings or Norwegian Vikings. They simply called them "men from the North"—Norsemen or Northmen. A popular prayer in the 9th century was "From the fury of the Northmen, deliver us, O Lord." The early Vikings themselves identified with their local districts, calling themselves "men of Hardanger" or "men of Vestfold." Only toward the end of the Viking Age did a concept of national identity begin to develop.

VIKING LIFE   Historians tell us that many Viking settlements were based on trade, were well organized, and had a high level of architecture and artistry. They had law assemblies that convened once a year to settle disputes and make important decisions, although additional assemblies could be called to settle disputes. Anyone could convene an assembly by sending an arrow to a neighboring farm. One man was selected to memorize the laws and was required to answer anyone who asked legal questions by reciting the laws at the assembly.

VIKING WOMEN   Women did the household jobs—mainly cooking, spinning, and weaving—with the help of thralls, or slaves. They also taught their children by telling them stories and riddles, in this way passing on their traditions. Viking stories of their heroes, called sagas, were not written down until the 13th century.

There was somewhat more equality between the sexes in the Viking communities than in the rest of Europe at the time. Viking women could own property, could divorce their husbands, and were in charge when the men were away. A wife's symbol of authority was the key to the storage chest that she carried fastened to her belt. The laws from the Viking Age make a distinction between free persons and slaves, but not between men and women. Many Norwegians see a connection between women's strong position during the Viking times and their strong position in Norway today. Norway has had an Equal Status Act—equivalent to an Equal Rights Amendment—since 1976.

Two Norwegian youths dressed as Vikings show how horns were blown to announce the return of a raiding expedition.

ONE NORWAY

Olav Tryggvason became
Olav I in 995.

Harald Fairhair (ruled c. 872–930) united most of western Norway after the Battle of Hafrsfjord in 872. (Some historians say it was in 892.) His son

Erik Bloodaxe, so called because he murdered seven of his eight brothers, ruled in 930–945 and was succeeded by his surviving brother Haakon. Haakon was Norway's first missionary king, but his efforts failed and he died in battle. Conflict erupted among his heirs, and many regional leaders refused to give up their independence. Sweden and Denmark took advantage of this unrest to gain territory in Norway.

UNDER DANISH RULE In 995, Olav Tryggvason (ruled 995–1000), a descendant of Harald Fairhair who had been brought up in England and baptized as a Catholic, ascended the throne. Olav I forced Catholicism on the Norwegians, killing those who would not accept it. This led Norwegian leaders to ally themselves with the Swedes and Danes to defeat and kill Olav I at the naval Battle of Svold. The victors divided the land among themselves.

In 1015, another descendant of Harald Fairhair, Olav Haraldsson (ruled 1015–1030), drove out the foreigners, reunited Norway, and was acknowledged as King Olav II throughout Norway. He continued the Christianization of Norway using the same methods as Olav I. As his power grew, he made many enemies among the nobles, who conspired with Canute II of Denmark. Olav II died in 1030 at the Battle of Stiklestad. His death put Norway into Danish hands.

Discontented with Canute's rule, the Norwegians began to think of Olav II as a hero despite his forced Christianization. A year after his death, he was proclaimed a saint by the Roman Catholic Church. St. Olav became the patron saint of Norway, and Christianity was firmly rooted in the country. When Canute II died in 1035, Olav II's son Magnus was proclaimed Norway's king. Magnus I united Norway and Denmark under his rule in 1047. For the next three centuries, Norwegian kings ruled Norway.

AGE OF GREATNESS

Haakon IV's accession to the throne (ruled 1217–1263) ended a conflict between church and state that began in 1196 and escalated into civil war. He reunited the country and made peace with the church. He accepted a new rule of succession whereby the throne would pass to the eldest son.

Canute II of Denmark was also called Canute the Great because he made many wise laws.

Haakon IV's reign is known as the Age of Greatness. He reorganized the government and maintained diplomatic contacts with many countries, including France and England. Under Haakon IV, the kingdom of Norway included all the western islands in the North Atlantic, and mainland Norway contained three regions that are now part of Sweden. Haakon IV also formally annexed Greenland in 1261 and Iceland in 1262.

Akershus Fortress in Oslo was built during the reign of Haakon V. The king had several fortresses built because the kingdom's naval defenses were weak.

Haakon was succeeded by his son Magnus Lagabøte. Magnus (Haakon V) revised the laws and persuaded the legislative assemblies to accept a common law for the whole country. When Norway's overseas possessions became hard to defend, Magnus sold the Hebrides and the Isle of Man to Scotland in 1266. This loss of territory signaled the decline of Norway.

UNDER SWEDISH RULE

In 1319, Haakon V died without male heirs. The throne went to the son of his daughter, who had married a Swedish prince. Thus Norway came under Swedish rule. Magnus VII lived in Sweden and neglected Norway.

After the bubonic plague killed half of Norway's population in 1350, the people demanded more consideration of their needs. To satisfy their demands, Magnus VII abdicated in favor of his son Haakon in 1355. Haakon VI was to be the last king of an independent Norway until 1905.

THE KALMAR UNION

Haakon VI's consort, Queen Margrete, who was also queen of Denmark, became queen of Norway when he died in 1380. In 1397, after Swedish nobles elected her to rule their country, Queen Margrete formally united Sweden, Denmark, and Norway under the Kalmar Union. Sweden broke away from the union in 1523, but Norway remained under the Danes for the next four centuries. In 1536, Denmark declared Norway a Danish province, and Norwegians lost the right to influence their country's affairs.

BACK TO SWEDEN

During the Napoleonic Wars of 1804–1814, Denmark allied itself with France. Britain set up a blockade to prevent ships with supplies from reaching Norway, and the people there suffered. Denmark, defeated by Sweden in 1813, ceded Norway to Sweden in the Treaty of Kiel, but kept Norway's island colonies, Iceland, Greenland, and the Faeroe Islands.

Norway refused to recognize the treaty and declared its independence, adopting a Norwegian constitution on May 17, 1814. Sweden refused to accept this action and attacked and subdued Norwegian troops. In November 1814, the Norwegian parliament accepted King Charles XIII of Sweden as Norway's ruler, and he promised to uphold Norway's constitution. The two countries were to have one king and be allied in war, but in all other respects they were to be independent of each other in full equality. Under the union with Sweden, Norway was granted self-government.

The Norwegian constitution adopted elements of the U.S. Constitution, the French Constitution of 1791, and constitutional practices in England. It established the principle of the sovereignty of the people and the separation of powers among an executive, a judiciary, and a legislature.

King Haakon VII, Queen Maud, and Crown Prince Olav in 1910. Thirty years later, during World War II, King Haakon VII's stand inspired Norwegians and stiffened their will to resist the Germans. He became a symbol of resistance throughout the war, and during the long days of the German occupation the letter H and the number 7 appeared on mountainsides, snowbanks, and city walls.

INDEPENDENT NORWAY

The economy in the last few decades of the 19th century was good but it could not keep pace with the population growth. Between 1866 and 1915, more than 600,000 Norwegians emigrated to North America. This prompted democratic reforms. The right to vote was extended to all men over 25 in 1898, and to women over 25 in 1913.

The independence movement had been growing in Norway, and in 1892 negotiations began on the terms of the Swedish-Norwegian union. These proved fruitless, and in 1905, the entire Norwegian cabinet resigned. As Norway's constitution only allowed the king to rule through the cabinet, this left the Swedish king helpless. Norway no longer had a king; therefore the union between Norway and Sweden no longer existed. Sweden initially refused to dissolve the union but finally agreed to put the matter to a vote in Norway. Norwegians voted almost unanimously for independence, and Sweden recognized Norway as an independent country in September 1905.

The Norwegians voted to establish a constitutional monarchy, and elected Prince Carl of Denmark as their king. He became King Haakon VII of Norway, the first king of Norway since the death of Haakon VI in 1380. He ruled Norway until his death in 1957.

WORLD WAR II

Tensions escalated in Europe during the 1930s. As it had done in World War I, Norway maintained a stance of neutrality. Its neutrality was of little significance when war broke out, however, as Germany and Britain recognized Norway's strategic importance. From bases on its coasts, German submarines would be able to operate in the North Sea. Realizing this, on April 8, 1940, the Allies announced that the British Navy had mined the coast. Norway protested, but soon had worse things to worry about.

THE GERMANS ARE COMING Before dawn on April 9, 1940, the Germans invaded Norway and Denmark in a brilliantly executed surprise attack. Denmark capitulated in a few hours. Norway decided to fight, even though the Germans had superior numbers and firepower. In the Oslofjord, Norway's old guns and torpedoes sank a large cruiser with 160,000 Germans aboard. The Germans were delayed for a few crucial hours, and in that time King Haakon VII and the members of the cabinet and the parliament left Oslo by train for Hamar, 80 miles (129 kilometers) north. The Bank of Norway's 50 tons of gold was also on its way north by the time the Germans overcame Norway's resistance.

The parliament met in Elverum and unanimously decided that the government should have full powers to act for the nation, even if the king and cabinet were on foreign soil. The Germans demanded that Norway surrender and that King Haakon appoint the founder of the Norwegian Nazi party, Vidkun Quisling, prime minister. The king declared he would rather abdicate. When the Germans started bombing, the officials hid in the woods nearby. The king and the cabinet fled north, keeping just ahead of the Germans. On May 1, the provisional capital was set up in the northern city of Tromsø.

In December 1942, U.S. President Franklin D. Roosevelt called Norway "conquered and unconquerable." He added, "If there is anyone who still wonders why this war is being fought, let him look to Norway.... If there is anyone who doubts the democratic will to win, again I say, let him look to Norway."

The Germans occupied Norway from 1940 until 1945.

GERMAN OCCUPATION Norway fought for two months against the Germans but finally fell and was occupied until Germany's surrender in 1945. Membership in the Nazi party increased from a few thousand in August 1940 to 43,000 in 1943 due to constant pressure to join.

Norwegians expressed their resistance to the German occupation in many ways. Some wore paper clips, a Norwegian invention, on their cuffs or lapels. Others wore flowers in their lapels on patriotic occasions. Many refused to ride buses where they would have to sit next to Germans or Norwegian Nazi party members. Some hid radios to listen to BBC (Britain's official station) broadcasts, and some helped write and distribute underground newspapers. By 1943, Norway had 60 underground newspapers.

Almost half of Norway's small Jewish population escaped the Nazis. Of the approximately 1,400 Norwegian Jews and 200 Jewish refugees from central Europe, 763 were deported to Auschwitz and other death camps. Only 24 of the deported Jews survived.

POSTWAR PERIOD

Germany lost the war, and Norway was liberated on May 8, 1945. King Haakon VII returned home to a big welcome. Twenty-four Norwegian collaborators, including Vidkun Quisling, were sentenced to death, and 19,000 others were imprisoned. Conflicts broke out between the Soviet Union and the Western nations almost immediately after World War II. Norway was anxious because it shared a border with the Soviet Union. Having learned that it could not rely on neutrality, Norway joined the North Atlantic Treaty Organization (NATO) in April 1949.

Norway had been left impoverished because no trade was carried on during the war. An acute housing shortage existed because no building was carried on either and because retreating German troops had destroyed many buildings. The government gave priority to restoring Norway's productive capacity in consumer goods. By 1953, the north had been rebuilt and hydroelectric power had increased by 50%.

Vidkun Quisling gave the English language a new word—"quisling," meaning someone who undermines his or her country from within.

SABOTAGE!

Norwegians mounted many acts of resistance against the Germans, from wearing King Haakon VII's emblem to running the Shetland Bus Service that ferried escapees to Scotland and carried weapons, radios, and special agents to Norway.

An act of sabotage that possibly affected the outcome of the war was the destruction of the heavy water (deuterium oxide) plant at Rjukan in Telemark. Heavy water is used in building atomic bombs, and Germany needed this plant in its race against the United States to build the first atomic bomb. On February 27, 1943, nine Norwegians climbed down a steep, icy mountainside, crossed a river, and climbed another mountain to the heavily guarded factory. Eluding guards, they broke in, poured out the deuterium oxide, and planted explosives. Four of the nine remained safely hidden on Hardanger Plateau while the Germans mounted an extensive search for the culprits, and the others skied 250 miles (402 kilometers) to safety in Sweden.

GOVERNMENT

NORWAY IS a constitutional monarchy. The king is head of state, but his power is more symbolic than real. All three of Norway's kings since independence in 1905 have played a quiet role in government, privately questioning government leaders but refraining from public statements on policy.

THE MONARCHY

The king of Norway is a symbol of national unity. He is also the supreme commander of the Norwegian armed forces, and the head of the Church of Norway.

Norway has been blessed with three kind, thoughtful, humble, and good kings since the country's independence from Sweden in 1905. At that time, Norway elected Prince Carl of Denmark as their king. He became King Haakon VII of Norway, the first king of Norway since the death of Haakon VI in 1380. By taking the name Haakon, he continued the line that had ended with the death of Haakon VI. King Haakon VII took as his motto, "My all for Norway," and the two kings who came after him have the same motto.

King Olav V (ruled 1957–1991) succeeded King Haakon VII. Already a respected resistance hero, he soon became admired for his hard work and humble demeanor. Norwegians have met him skiing outside Oslo without bodyguards. During the oil crisis in 1972, when the nation was asked to conserve fuel, King Olav set a personal example by taking the trolley to go skiing and insisting on paying his fare. He held a special place in the hearts of Norwegians because he made his weaknesses public.

King Olav V was a navy man and a keen sailor. He is remembered fondly as "the people's king."

Opposite: **A guard at his post at Castle Park in Oslo.**

37

He explained to the people of Norway that he suffered from dyslexia, which caused him some trouble when he had to give speeches. Because he had made his handicap public, the people saw his difficulty as a symbol of human strength.

In 1991, King Harald V, the present king of Norway, succeeded to the throne. The health of the environment is a passion for King Harald. He was president of the World Wildlife Fund before becoming king and often stresses the serious need for worldwide conservation of the environment and Norway's special responsibility as a country with untouched wilderness areas.

THE ROLE OF THE ROYAL FAMILY

Royal succession in Norway had been in the direct male line, but the rule changed in 1990 to permit women to inherit the crown. After Crown Prince Haakon Magnus, who was born in 1973, the succession will pass to his first child, regardless of gender.

Above and opposite: **King Harald V and Queen Sonja Haraldsen. Like his father, King Harald is an expert sailor.**

In addition to royal duties and political affairs, the royal family has always been active in sports, especially skiing and sailing, and also very involved in social concerns. Princess Martha Louise was appointed a goodwill ambassador by the United Nations High Commissioner for Refugees in 1991. King Olav, despite the traditional royal reluctance to make public statements to influence policy, made a strong statement in 1987 in favor of maintaining an open society for the increasing stream of refugees into Norway. He reminded the country that he too had been an immigrant—arriving in Norway as a two-year-old when most of his family were abroad.

The royal family has had a strong tradition of being close to the people. Although some Norwegians see the monarchy as a contradiction of the ideal of equality, others point out that the king was elected in 1905. Until 1935, however, the Labor government of Norway was unfriendly to the royal family, often refusing to pass the palace budget or to attend dinner parties with the king.

World War II was a turning point in the acceptance of the royal family, as Norwegians were impressed with the courage of King Haakon VII in refusing German demands, and the future King Olav's bravery during the resistance. A measure of the royal family's acceptance is that in 1990, when a proposal to make Norway a republic was introduced in parliament, it received only 19 votes from the 165-member parliament. Today, over 90% of Norwegians approve of the royal family.

QUEENS OF NORWAY

From 1938 to 1991, Norway was without a queen. Queen Maud, wife of King Haakon VII, had been frail most of her life. She was the daughter of King Edward VII and Queen Alexandra of Great Britain. Crown Princess Martha, King Olav's Swedish-born wife, then assumed the duties of the queen of Norway, but she died in 1954, before her husband succeeded to the throne. Having been without a queen since 1938, Norwegians were particularly happy when Sonja Haraldsen, a commoner, married Crown Prince Harald and, in 1991, became Norway's first Norwegian-born queen when her husband succeeded to the throne.

ADMINISTRATIVE DIVISIONS

Norway is divided into 19 *fylker* ("FEWL-ker"), or counties. The city of Oslo is a *fylker* on its own. Each *fylker* except Oslo has a governor appointed by the king. The *fylker* are further divided into rural and urban *kommuner* ("koo-MEW-ner"), or districts. Community councils, elected every four years, run the local districts. Each *fylker* also has a county council consisting of members of the community councils.

THE STORTING

Norway's Storting (parliament) building was constructed over six years, from 1861 to 1866.

Norway's 165-member parliament is called the Storting ("stoor-TING"). Only the Storting has the power to enact and repeal laws, amend the constitution, impose taxes, appropriate money for government expenses, and keep a check on government agencies. It also appoints the Nobel Peace Prize committee.

Members of the Storting are elected every four years as representatives of their counties and political parties. Alternates are also elected, in case the elected member dies, is absent, or becomes a member of the cabinet.

All Norwegian citizens 18 years old and older can vote in parliamentary elections. Each of Norway's 19 counties elects four to 16 Storting members, depending on the size of the local population.

THE NOBEL PEACE PRIZE

Since 1901, the Nobel Peace Prize committee at the Nobel Institute in Oslo, which consists of five members appointed by the Storting, has announced the winner of this prestigious award. The Nobel Peace Prize is given to "the person, or body, who has done the most or the best work for brotherhood among nations, for the abolition or reduction of standing armies, and for the holding and promotion of peace congresses."

Alfred Nobel, the Swedish inventor of dynamite, stipulated in his will of 1895 that the Nobel prizes in the sciences and for literature should be awarded by Swedish institutions, but that the decision on the peace prize should be left to a committee appointed by the Norwegian parliament. Although Norway and Sweden were still united at his death, Nobel's stipulation may have reflected his knowledge that the Norwegians were early supporters of the principle of international arbitration.

The Nobel Peace Prize committee is an independent body whose members are not usually members of the Storting. The committee considers nominations from peace organizations, previous winners, and various other groups. In recent years, nominations have averaged 100 a year. The committee may refrain from awarding the prize altogether (it has done so 19 times), may give the prize to one person or institution, or award a joint prize. Several awards have been controversial, including the committee's decision in 1990 to award the prize to Mikhail Gorbachev, which provoked another Norwegian group to award a People's Peace Prize to Lithuanian President Vytautas Landsbergis. Another controversy arose in 1994 when most of the committee decided to award the prize jointly to Moshe Aaron, former president of Israel, Israeli President Yitzhak Rabin, and Palestinian leader Yasser Arafat. Yasser Arafat's inclusion was the contentious issue, and one member of the committee threatened to resign if he was awarded the prize on the grounds that Arafat had engaged in terrorist activities. The issue was finally resolved, and the three men were jointly awarded the prestigious Nobel Peace Prize for their work in resolving the crisis between Israel and the Palestinians.

The Storting has only one house, but its members divide themselves into two sections—one-third sit on the Lagting ("LAHG-ting," or law assembly) and two-thirds on the Odelsting ("OH-duhls-ting," or heritage of the people assembly)—to debate and vote on proposed legislation. A bill is first considered in the Odelsting, and it is considered for a second time in the Lagting. To become law, a bill must be passed by both bodies in succession and signed by the king when meeting with the cabinet. If the two bodies cannot agree on a bill, it can be passed by two-thirds of the Storting and then sent to the king to be signed into law.

THE CABINET

The cabinet consists of the prime minister and several other ministers (currently 18). Most cabinet ministers head a government department such as Foreign Affairs, the Environment, or Church and Cultural Affairs. Cabinet members cannot be members of the Storting, but may be called upon by the Storting to answer questions from the floor. Cabinet appointments must be approved by the Storting and usually reflect its political composition.

The cabinet meets several times a week. It is generally thought that the Norwegian prime minister, though having considerable influence, has less power than the U.S. president or the British or Canadian prime minister.

When the United Nations established the World Commission on Environment and Development in 1983, it was headed by Norway's first woman prime minister, Gro Harlem Brundtland (right).

A WOMEN'S POLITICAL CHRONOLOGY

1884 – The Norwegian Association for the Rights of Women is founded. It works for improvement in women's education and of the legal status of married women.

1907 – Norwegian women get limited suffrage in parliamentary elections. All women who pay taxes, or whose husbands pay taxes, may vote.

1911 – Anna Rogstadt becomes the first woman member of the Storting.

1913 – Norwegian women are given the right to vote in national elections. Norway is the second country in Europe, after Finland, to extend voting rights to women.

1956 – Elva Kolstad becomes president of the Norwegian Association for the Rights of Women, a position she will hold until 1986.

1960 – Signer Ryssdale becomes Norway's first woman counselor at law.

1970 – Ragnhild Selmer becomes Norway's first woman Supreme Court judge.

1971 – Inger Valle becomes Minister of Family and Consumer Affairs.

1972 – Inger Valle becomes Minister of Government Administration and Elva Kolstad becomes Minister of Consumer Affairs.

1974 – Elva Kolstad becomes president of the now disbanded Liberal Party.

1976 – Major Eva Berg becomes chief of the Joint Norwegian Military Nursing Services. Gro Harlem Brundtland becomes Minister of the Environment. Ruth Ryste becomes Minister of Social Affairs. Annemarie Lorentzen becomes Minister of Consumer Affairs and Government Administration. Inger Valle becomes Minister of Justice.

1979 – Norway's Equal Status Act prohibits sexual discrimination in all but religious communities.

1981 – Gro Harlem Brundtland becomes Norway's first woman prime minister.

1986 – Gro Harlem Brundtland is reelected as prime minister.

1988 – The Equal Status Act is amended to require that the percentage of women on all publicly appointed committees and boards must be at least 40%.

1990 – Gro Harlem Brundtland is reelected as prime minister.

1990s – The three major political parties, Labor, Center, and Conservative, are headed by women.

Norway has always been ahead of the times with regard to women's rights, both in the social sphere and in politics. The first women's suffrage organization in Norway was created in 1885, a year after the founding of the first women's rights association. In 1986, 44% of the ministers in the Norwegian cabinet were women.

Trygve Lie, Norway's foreign minister during World War II, was working out of London since Norway was occupied by the Germans. In London, he established cordial relations with the British, Americans, and Russians. He influenced the Norwegian government's decision to change its policy of neutrality to one of cooperation with Atlantic countries.

POLITICAL PARTIES

Norway has several political parties. The Labor Party has been the largest and most often in power since 1927 but faces increasing opposition by the Conservatives, who are often allied with the Center Party (formerly the Farmer's Party) and the Christian Democrats. Other parties in Norway include the Socialist Left and the Party of Progress.

Although the Labor Party has traditionally been the party in power, there has recently been a shift in favor of the Socialist Left Party, from those dissatisfied with labor due to the rise in unemployment, and in favor of the Party of Progress, from those dissatisfied with Norway's refugee policy, high taxation, and heavy investment in social welfare. These shifts have made it increasingly difficult to form stable cabinets because the ruling party must build cabinets through coalitions.

INTERNATIONAL COOPERATION

Norway has a tradition of active participation in international organizations that promote peaceful cooperation, including the League of Nations, its successor the United Nations, and the Nordic Council. Norwegians who have served include Fridtjof Nansen (1861–1930), the League of Nations' High Commissioner for Prisoners of War; Trygve Lie (1896–1968), the first United Nations secretary-general, serving from 1946 to 1953; and Gro

Harlem Brundtland, who was made chairperson of the World Commission on Environment and Development in 1983.

Since 1983, Norway has contributed at least 1% of its Gross Domestic Product (GDP) to development aid, which is much higher than the average contribution of 0.35% made by other industrialized Western countries and the United Nations' suggested 0.7%. Norway's contribution is regularly reviewed to ensure that it improves the situation of women and that it supports sustainable development—development that is ecologically benign and follows the guidelines of the World Commission on Environment and Development.

Norway is one of the four countries that keeps a permanent force of soldiers ready for U.N. peacekeeping missions and has participated in all of them. Norway has also been active in the Nordic Council since the council's founding in 1952. The council coordinates cultural exchange, research, and social welfare benefits among Denmark, Finland, Iceland, Norway, and Sweden. One of the council's most significant results is the freedom of people of member countries to travel within the countries without passports and the freedom to work and reside in any of the five countries without work or resident permits.

With almost all other European nations joining the European Union, Norway is in danger of being isolated in terms of trade agreements, political clout, and other benefits that might accrue from being part of a larger economic entity.

THE EUROPEAN UNION

In 1994, despite active campaigning in favor of joining the European Union (EU) by the prime minister and other government officials, Norwegians voted not to join the EU. Norwegians feel that Norway is doing well as an independent country, and they see no need to join forces with the other European countries. Indeed, Norway has had bad experiences with political unions in its long history, and this may be one reason why its people are reluctant to enter into another.

45

ECONOMY

SINCE WORLD WAR II, Norway's economy has undergone rapid industrial growth. The development of hydroelectric power and the discovery of oil in the 1960s have been instrumental in Norway's economic expansion. Although the economy slowed somewhat in the 1980s, Norwegians continue to enjoy one of the highest standards of living in the world.

The economy is dominated by private enterprise, but strict state regulations affect the private sector. The government regulates the disposal of industrial waste and supervises the activities of banks and insurance companies.

The Norwegian economy has undergone major changes in the past decade. The traditional industrial and manufacturing sector has declined, while the service sector and modern industries, such as the petroleum industry, engineering, and data technology, have expanded. Foreign trade accounts for about 42% of Norway's GDP, and service industries for about 39%. Norway's main trading partners include Britain, Sweden, Denmark, Germany, Japan, and the United States.

The Working Environment Act of 1977 requires employers to provide job security and limits working hours to nine hours a day. It also forbids laborers to work more than 200 hours of overtime per year. Norway enjoys a low unemployment rate compared to other countries.

Opposite: **A worker packs sardines in a factory in Stavanger. Norway is a leading exporter of fish and fish products.**

Below: **The potential energy of numerous waterfalls provides the basis of Norway's hydroelectric power.**

An offshore oil rig before it is towed out to sea. Small rigs, such as the one above, are used to drill wells at sea. When oil is discovered, a larger platform is established.

Opposite: This natural gas tanker is under construction near Stavanger.

OIL AND ENERGY

When Norway sought to extend its territorial waters, geologists testified during hearings in Geneva in 1958 that there was very little possibility of finding oil, gas, or sulfur along Norway's continental shelf. Not surprisingly, therefore, when a representative from Phillips Petroleum in Oklahoma approached Trygve Lie in 1962 about the possibility of prospecting for oil off Norway, he replied, "I believe you must have made a mistake ... Norway has no oil or gas." In 1969, Phillips Petroleum struck oil in what is now known as the Ekofisk oil fields in the Norwegian section of the North Sea. By 1975, Norway was exporting oil products. In 1986, revenues from oil accounted for nearly 20% of the GDP, despite a drop in oil prices.

Most of the current oil resources are located in the continental shelf off Norway's southwestern coast, but considerable reserves of oil are known to exist beyond the Arctic Circle. The government has announced plans to extend oil exploration into the Barents Sea.

The Norwegian government controls much of the oil industry. After the discovery of oil, the Storting voted to limit annual production to conserve the oil fields. In 1972, Statoil was created to oversee all aspects of the oil industry, from exploration to processing and the sale of petroleum and natural gas.

Only about 20% of crude oil is refined in Norway, but there are plans to extend the current refinery at Mongstad and build a huge complex at Kristo. Most of Norway's oil and gas are exported. Norway provides about 12% of western Europe's gas requirements. For its own energy, Norway relies heavily on hydroelectric power. Norway produces more hydroelectric power in relation to its population than any other country in the world.

THE NAMING OF OIL FIELDS

Norwegians draw on their rich heritage of Old Norse myths and folktales to name many of their oil fields. Northwest of Stavanger there is Odin; Frigg is on the median line between Britain and Norway. Near the Norway-Denmark divide is Valhalla, and Troll can be found northwest of Bergen.

Less familiar names are Heimdall, northwest of Stavanger, named for the Old Norse god who guarded the rainbow bridge Bifrost. Sleipner, close to Frigg, is named for Sleipne, Odin's fastest and eight-legged horse. Named for the goat that stood on the roof of Valhalla and from whose udders came the liquor the fallen warriors drank is Heidrun, off Nordland County. Gullfaks, west of the Sognefjord, is a ship in Norwegian folklore that can sail as fast on land as at sea. In Old Norse myths also a horse called Gullfaks belonged to the giant Rungne.

MANUFACTURING

Norway developed industries later than other European countries because it lacked coal to fuel factories. The development of hydroelectric power spurred rapid industrialization in the 20th century. Early industries depended on local raw materials, such as iron ore, timber, and fish. Since the discovery of oil in the late 1960s, a petrochemical industry has also developed.

Manufacturing contributes about 15% to the country's GDP. Almost half of Norway's factories are located near Oslo. In the 1980s, wage increases and economic conditions made Norway's products more expensive and therefore less competitive on the international market.

Norway is the largest exporter of metal in the world after Canada. Norway imports most of the raw materials it refines and exports them immediately. Norway is also one of the biggest producers and exporters of chemical products. Other manufactured products include machinery, pulp and paper, and textiles.

AGRICULTURE AND FORESTRY

Norway has only three main farming areas—in the southeast, the southwest, and in Trøndelag. These

A combine harvester works in a wheat field. As only 3–4% of Norway's land can be cultivated, the country has to import most of its grain.

areas have a relatively favorable climate, flat fields, and fertile soil. Although Norway has developed from a mainly agricultural country into an industrial one, the government was running homesteading programs to encourage new settlement on the land as recently as the 1950s.

Only 28% of all farmers are full-time farmers. There are about 94,700 farms in Norway, employing 6% of the work force. Most are dairy farms producing milk and cheese. The country produces enough livestock to meet its own needs and grows potatoes, barley, oats, and wheat. However, grain for bread is imported, along with sugar, vegetables, and fruit.

Norwegian farms are generally small: a typical farm has 22 acres (9 hectares) of arable land and 124 acres (50 hectares) of forest. Many farmers supplement their income by engaging in commercial forestry. Land owned by farmers contains about half the nation's productive forests, primarily in the counties of Nord-Trøndelag, Hedmark, Oppland, and Buskerud.

The government has traditionally subsidized farmers. The Storting decided in 1976 that all farmers should have the same annual income as an average industrial worker. However, these policies are being reviewed, and subsidies have been reduced. The government has promoted a policy of keeping people employed in all rural areas of the country to maintain Norway's ability to grow much of its food. As many of the government's agricultural policies are in conflict with the EU's regulations concerning farming, most farmers were against joining the EU.

Logs are floated down the Oslofjord. Most of Norway's timber is birch, pine, and spruce and is used in wood processing. Pulp and paper make up about 8% of Norway's export earnings. Logging is strictly regulated by the government, and the country imports timber from Sweden and Finland to meet the needs of its processing plants.

Norway has long ranked
among the world's
leading fishing nations.

FISHING

Providing almost 5% of the total global catch, Norway ranks as one of the world's top fishing countries, although the industry now earns less than 1% of Norway's GDP.

Norwegian fishing crews catch about 2.5 million tons of fish per year, including cod, capelin, coalfish, and shrimp. Most of the catch is processed and exported. Fish farming of salmon and trout in the fjords and coastal inlets has become an important component of the industry. Most of Norway's hatcheries are located in the counties of Hordaland, Møre og Romsdal, and Sør-Trøndelag.

Because they are in danger of extinction, the government strictly regulates or forbids fishing of herring and seals. Commercial whaling has been suspended to allow whales to replenish their numbers.

Oceanor, Norway's ocean-monitoring body, helped the fishing industry by developing a highly sensitive electronic sensor to detect and measure the presence of 85 different types of algae in the ocean. Algae bloom can devastate fish farms. In 1988, for example, sensors registered a dramatic increase in the growth of a toxic alga in the North Sea. Oceanor advised fish farmers to tow their installations into areas of fjords not affected by the alga, and this saved salmon stock worth more than $130 million that year.

SHIPPING

With a coastline 34,000 miles (55,000 kilometers) long, and a population concentrated along the coast, it is not surprising that Norway has a traditional involvement with ships and the sea. From catering to its own transport needs, the shipping industry in Norway has grown into the country's third largest export industry. Norway is the fourth biggest shipping nation after Liberia, Panama, and Greece.

The shipping industry suffered a depression in the 1970s, when oil prices rose. At the same time, developing countries, such as Panama and Liberia, became increasingly competitive and gained a growing share of the shipping market. The depression in shipping continued into the 1980s.

To meet the challenge, Norwegian shipping companies concentrated on new markets and operations that called for highly skilled maritime knowledge and also sharpened their marketing and consultancy skills. The Storting established the International Ship Register (NIS) in 1987 to assist shippers through a network of overseas stations.

A ship docks at a yard for repairs. In order to survive, many shipyards became smaller and more specialized.

53

A seaplane waits at a jetty at Geirangerfjord. Seaplanes are often used to transport people from the fjords to the mountains for hunting or other sport.

TRANSPORTATION

Despite its rugged terrain, Norway has developed an efficient network of roads, railways, and water routes. Public transportation is well developed, including intercity buses and streetcars within cities. Two-thirds of Norway's 55,000 miles (89,000 kilometers) of road are paved. Because of the terrain, many roads curve along fjords and mountains and pass through tunnels and over bridges. The Norwegian road network includes more than 500 tunnels.

Historically, Norwegians depended on water transport, which was more efficient than land transport, given Norway's physical geography.

Coastal passenger and car ferries provide a vital service for those living in western Norway, where roads are crisscrossed by fjords, and on the hundreds of islands.

Norway's rail system branches out from Oslo and connects all parts of the country. The railway extends to Sweden and Denmark. Norway has nearly 50 airports and relies increasingly on domestic airlines to cover the mountainous areas within the country.

A bridge in Tromsø. Although car density is high in Norway (2.2 inhabitants per car), highways and bridges are generally free of traffic jams.

NORWEGIANS

BY INTERNATIONAL STANDARDS, Norway has a small and homogeneous population. Only about 3% of the population is foreign born. The country has two indigenous ethnic minorities, the Norwegian Finns and the Sami.

NORWEGIANS

Most Norwegians are closely related to the Danes and the Swedes. The ancestors of these three Scandinavian peoples came from lands east of the Baltic Sea, from around the Mediterranean Sea, or from the European Alps. Over the centuries, Norwegians have intermarried with other groups.

Norwegians pride themselves on their strong traditions of equality and humanitarianism. They are also fiercely independent, an attitude fueled by centuries of domination by others.

Above and opposite: **Contrary to the popular image of all Norwegians being fair haired and blue eyed, many Norwegians have dark hair.**

NORWEGIAN FINNS

The Kvener, or Finns, were involved in trade in northern Norway from the early 12th century. From the early 18th century through the 19th, some Finns came to Norway, looking for a more secure life in the fjords of Troms and Finnmark. Some were escaping marauding Russians. Others were fleeing the Swedish wars and the famine years of the 1860s. The best known Kven center, Vadsø on the far eastern coast of Norway, was called Vesi-Saari in Finnish, meaning water island. In 1875, Finnish speakers made up 62% of the population, but today very little Finnish is heard in Norway. There are still about 12,000 Finnish speakers in Norway.

Above and opposite: **Sami man and woman herder.**

*"Our life
is like a ski track
on the white
plateau
which the wind
erases
before the day
breaks."*

—Paulus Utsi and
Inger Huuva-Utsi,
Sami poets and
reindeer drivers
(translated by
Harold Gaski)

THE SAMI

The Sami have lived in Norway, Sweden, Finland, and the Kola Peninsula for thousands of years. Originally from Asia, they are darker and shorter than most Norwegians. Their language is related to Finnish. About 30,000 Sami—two-thirds of all Sami—live in Norway. In 1989, the Sami parliament opened, giving Sami a voice in issues concerning their status in Norway.

More than half of the Norwegian Sami live in the northern county of Finnmark, which means Sami borderland. In Old Norse, the Sami were called Finner, indicating they were a people who could locate game and find their way in wild country. Traditionally, the Sami are nomads who follow herds of reindeer. Many modern Sami have settled in fishing and farming communities and are intermarrying with the Norwegians.

Like Native Americans, the Sami are eager for outsiders to see beyond the stereotypes based on museum displays and early travelers' accounts. The Romans recorded that the Sami dressed in animal skins and traveled on narrow pieces of wood, the earliest skis, and that Sami women hunted

REINDEER HERDING: A TRADITIONAL SAMI OCCUPATION

The life of the Sami reindeer-herding nomads has a regular pattern: a long stay at a winter base where herds feed on lichen under snow and on trees, a spring migration toward the coast with a pause for calving, travel to summer grazing areas on peninsulas and islands, and in the fall, a reindeer roundup before heading back to camp. Nomadic Sami live in *lavvo* ("LAH-voh"), traditional skin tents, and travel on skis, the most efficient way of traversing snowy areas.

Reindeer-herding Sami face serious obstacles because their traditional migration routes are threatened by dams, roads, national parks, sport fishing and hunting, mining, tourism, and military bases. Pollution is also a serious threat. The Chernobyl nuclear explosion affected the Sami living in Trøndelag, who were forced to slaughter their herds due to the high level of radioactivity.

The Alta-Kautokeino River hydroelectric project proposed in 1970 became a major test of Sami rights. Sami, environmentalists, and advocates for ethnic and minority rights agitated against the dam, which would affect traditional Sami migratory routes. Despite the high level of mobilization against the project, the Storting and the Supreme Court approved it in 1982.

alongside the men. In the 15th century, Norwegians began to invade Sami areas, depleting stocks of wild game. Some Sami responded by becoming full-time reindeer breeders and herders and organizing cooperatives based on kin ties. Others settled on the coast and continued hunting and fishing.

Only two-thirds of the Sami speak a Sami dialect, an unfortunate result of attempts by missionaries, agricultural experts, and schoolteachers from the 1850s to the 1950s to "Norwegianize" the Sami. In the 1960s, the official government position shifted to a policy of accommodation and support. Research projects focusing on Sami language and culture resulted in new curricula for all educational levels. Today, students may choose Sami as their first language in many communities. The Sami themselves have become involved in this Sami revivalism. There are now Sami newspapers, a Sami radio station, a major research library housed in Karasjok, and museums and theater groups.

THE ROLE OF WOMEN

Traditionally, Norwegian women fended for themselves and made their own decisions. In many rural communities, the men used to go fishing off the coast for several months, leaving the women to run the farms and local affairs. This pattern continues today, with the men going off to work on oil rigs for two to three weeks at a time before returning home for a couple of weeks—except that today there are also women working on the rigs, and most women onshore are no longer on the farms.

Even though Norway was the second country to give women the right to vote in national elections, and the first woman to sit in the Storting was Anna Rogstadt in 1911, no woman had been a cabinet minister until 1945, when Kirsten Hansteen was given the title of consultant minister without a department to run.

Norwegian women entered the paid work force later than other Scandinavian women. Even with the Equal Status Act,

A cruise officer from a ship touring Svalbard presents an image of cool efficiency.

there are differences in pay and major discrepancies in the sharing of housework in Norway today. Many women have also traditionally chosen to be educated within the caring professions such as public health and social welfare, whereas more men have acquired economic and technical skills. This has given rise to strong patterns of occupational segregation. Few women hold high-level jobs in industry or banking.

Norway established the world's first Department of Women's Law at the University of Oslo. A major secretariat for women and research sponsors studies of issues that affect and concern women.

EMIGRATION TO THE UNITED STATES

From 1840 until World War I, a growing flood of emigrants left Norway for the New World. Most emigrated because of rural poverty, leaving behind them small cottages that have been called starvation cottages. Many were farm laborers who were paid only a few pennies a day, or children of farmers whose plots were too small or infertile to support an extended family.

Before the U.S. Immigration Act of 1924 restricted the flow of refugees, more than 800,000 Norwegians had emigrated to the United States. In 1882 alone, 28,628 Norwegians emigrated. No other country, except Ireland, had larger numbers of its people emigrate to the United States.

Most of the immigrants settled in New York, California, and farming communities in the Midwest. Life in the early years was hard for these immigrants, but Norwegian-language newspapers, churches, and cultural associations helped keep the communities together. In Minnesota, at least two private colleges have Norwegian roots: St. Olaf College and Luther College.

A number of private and public organizations have been founded to help Americans interested in researching their family history and lineage. Today, there are almost as many people of Norwegian descent living in the United States as there are Norwegians in Norway.

Although there had been some emigration of Norwegians to the early colonies in North America, the beginning of Norwegian emigration to the United States is dated from 1825, when the Restoration *carried 52 Norwegians from Stavanger to New York.*

FRIDTJOF NANSEN

Fridtjof Nansen led the Norwegian delegation in Geneva from the first League of Nations' session in 1920 until his death and played a heroic role in the bitter decade after World War I. He took on the assignment of League of Nations High Commissioner for Prisoners of War and administered the repatriation of 450,000 former prisoners of war.

Nansen also took on the even heavier burden of bringing relief to the millions of refugees and displaced persons uprooted in Europe and Asia during the war. When refugees could not cross international borders because they lacked proper identification documents, Nansen introduced a new form of supranational passport, the "Nansen passport," which he persuaded more than 50 governments to recognize. He also persuaded them to accept quotas of refugees.

When Nansen was awarded the Nobel Peace Prize for his achievements in refugee relief in 1922, he was already in the midst of another assignment. At the request of the International Committee of the Red Cross, he personally led an immense famine-relief operation in the Soviet Union from 1921 to 1923. When the League did not support the project, he contributed the funds from his peace prize. Most diplomats said the task was impossible. Starting with tons of Norwegian cod-liver oil, Nansen saved more than 7 million people, 6 million of them children, although he was deeply affected by the fact that thousands of others died.

Probably the greatest single achievement of Nansen's refugee work was the resettlement and exchange of several hundred thousand Greeks and Turks who fled to Greece following the defeat of the Greek Army in 1922. This rescue operation took eight years to accomplish and involved building new villages and industries for the resettled Greeks and Turks. His last project was particularly difficult—trying to assist the resettlement of Armenians.

NORWEGIAN NEWCOMERS

Foreigners amount to only about 3% of the total population of Norway. The majority are from the other Scandinavian countries. About 40% of immigrants are from outside Europe, especially from Asia. In the 1960s, Norway accepted migrant workers from Pakistan, India, Turkey, and Morocco. Since 1975, however, the government has placed a ban on immigration.

Norway still has a strong tradition of offering a place to asylum seekers and refugees. The country received a large increase in asylum seekers in the late 1980s, as other European countries began restricting the entry of political asylum seekers. Many came from Chile, Iran, Sri Lanka, the former Yugoslavia, Poland, and Somalia. Norway also was accepting between

1,000 and 4,000 refugees through the UN High Commission for Refugees, mostly from Iran and Vietnam. Although almost all were accepted in 1987, the acceptance rate has since dropped.

Norway provides schooling in the foreigner's native language as long as four people are interested, but newcomers are expected to learn Norwegian. Those of school age are expected to attend school. Others are integrated through work programs and Norwegian language classes. Most immigrants live in Oslo or near Bergen and Stavanger.

In spite of Norway's strong humanitarian tradition, many Norwegians are unhappy with the foreign-born population and overestimate its impact on society. Some foreigners have experienced discrimination. The government, media, and the royal family are trying to combat the hostility, and the immigrants themselves have formed associations to celebrate their cultural heritage and educate others.

Immigrants are given free lessons in the Norwegian language to help them adjust to the country.

LIFESTYLE

NORWAY ENJOYS one of the highest living standards in the world. There is very little discrepancy in income because the taxation system takes from the wealthy and gives to the not-so-wealthy. This has resulted in a fairly equitable society where most people are in the same economic class.

WORK

Norwegians are a hardworking people who also know where their priorities lie. Norway's parliament passed a Worker's Protection Act that limits maximum working hours to an annual average of nine hours a day. All night work is prohibited for day workers, as is work on Sundays and public holidays.

Like all other workers in Norway, rope makers in Bergen are protected by legislation.

Opposite: **Young street performers earn a little extra to stretch their allowance.**

Child labor is strictly controlled, and children under the age of 15 are allowed only light work, such as that of messengers. Those under the age of 18 are not permitted to work overtime or at night.

Usual business hours are from 8 a.m. to 4 p.m., with only a short break of about 20 minutes for lunch, usually of sandwiches brought from home. These working hours are faithfully followed in winter, but in summer, office workers often quit work an hour early in order to enjoy the sun as much as possible. Norway has also legislated a four-week vacation with full pay for all workers. This means a lot of time for family activities and leisure pursuits. Balancing family time and work is a deliberate policy in Norway. Working women are entitled to 33 weeks maternity leave with full wages, and working fathers are entitled to two weeks paternity leave.

Every family member is protected by a comprehensive package of health and welfare benefits.

A WELFARE NATION

Norway is a world leader in state-funded health care, housing, employment benefits, retirement plans, and other services. Norwegian laws guarantee the right to employment, a place to live, education, social security, and health and hospital benefits. The welfare system is funded through taxes and insurance. Recently, however, there has been discontent with the high level of taxation and Norwegians have begun to question whether they want to keep subsidizing lower-income families, usually immigrants.

Families with children under 16 receive a yearly allowance per child after the first. Aid is also available to help these families pay for housing. This has ensured a minimum standard of living for all Norwegian citizens.

Norwegians are required to buy into the national insurance program, which includes retirement funds, job retraining, and unemployment benefits. Free medical care and disability benefits are part of the plan. The cost of the program is borne jointly by workers, employers, and national and local governments.

A SPECIAL PLACE FOR CHILDREN WITH DISABILITIES

Norway has made special provisions for disabled children. The official educational policy is to integrate children of all capabilities into the regular educational system rather than stigmatizing those who are differently abled by segregating them. Differently abled children are encouraged to join in normal classes, usually with a therapist present. This is in line with Norway's policy to ensure equal educational opportunities for all.

This integration has helped able-bodied Norwegian children to learn to be patient and to appreciate their differently abled classmates. However, this integration may come at the expense of exceptionally gifted children. Norway's equal educational opportunities policy means that slow learners are given a helping hand, but gifted children are not given the opportunity to excel and develop at an accelerated pace.

Norway has realized that a balance between the needs of the disabled and those of the gifted is necessary and is striving toward an equilibrium.

HEALTH

Norway has no severe health problems apart from those common to wealthy countries, namely heart disease and cancer. Children receive a program of vaccinations, and everyone undergoes periodic tests for tuberculosis.

In the 1990s, life expectancy for Norwegians is 76 years, a gain of almost 25 years over their ancestors in the 1890s, who could only expect to live for 52 years. Norway also has one of the lowest infant mortality rates in the world, at 7.8 deaths out of every 100 babies born. Norway is experiencing a shortage of retirement and nursing homes because more Norwegians are living longer. The country is also experiencing a very low birth rate, a condition found in most industrialized countries. Women who choose to have children opt for small families of one or two children. At this rate, officials predict it will take more than 300 years for the country's population to double.

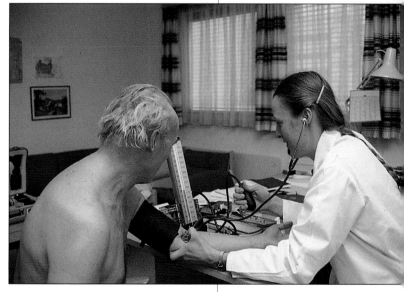

A doctor takes a reading of her patient's blood pressure. Health services in Norway are partly financed through compulsory membership of all Norwegians in the national insurance scheme.

67

If this little girl does not like the name her parents gave her, she can change it. Norwegian law has made it easy for people to change their names—once.

BIRTH AND BAPTISM

Although women do go to clinics for prenatal care before their baby is born, it is a midwife who helps them through the nine months of pregnancy. When the time comes for the baby to be born, the midwife accompanies the woman to the hospital and turns her over to the hospital midwife, who supervises the birth. New mothers are not pampered in Norway—childbirth is seen as a difficult procedure, not a debilitating ordeal.

One of the first ceremonies a child undergoes is baptism. Baptism marks the child's entry into the Church of Norway, the state religion since 1539. Family and close friends are usually invited, and two married couples are selected as the child's godparents. Theirs is a lifelong task as they are expected to be the child's moral guides, to ensure that he or she grows up with sound values and tolerant attitudes.

Baptism is also the ceremony at which a child is named. Naming a child in Norway used to follow a strict pattern. The eldest son was named after his paternal grandfather, and the next son after his maternal grandfather. The eldest and second daughters were named after their paternal and maternal grandmothers, respectively. Then the names of great-grandparents were used, or relatives who had passed away. Today, however, Norwegians are free to choose their children's names. They may make the selection from a book of names, or name their children after friends or relatives. Often, a child is given a grandparent's name as his or her middle name.

CONFIRMATION

One of the most important ceremonies for Norwegians who belong to the Church of Norway, confirmation represents the 14- or 15-year-old's acceptance of a Christian heritage and the principles of the Lutheran Church.

All those wishing to be confirmed attend a two-month preparatory course, during which they are given a thorough grounding in the principles of the church. If they decide they can abide by these principles, they then go through the confirmation ceremony, in which they publicly declare that they wish to remain a part of the Lutheran Church. The confirmation ceremony takes place in church and is attended by friends and family. There is usually a large celebration after the ceremony, and friends and relatives come from all over to participate and celebrate with the family.

THE *KVINNEGRUPPE*

The *kvinnegruppe* ("KVIN-nuh-GREW-puh") is a gathering of women interested in discussing women's issues and current literature. Members are mostly professional women in their mid-20s to mid-30s, although many are homemakers and university students. These women are not radical feminists, but are simply women interested in airing their opinions about the policies and issues that affect them. The group is not action-oriented, but it does serve as an outlet for women to discuss matters that concern them and listen to alternative points of view or gain support for their views. It is also a wonderful opportunity for interaction with like-minded women, and most members enjoy relaxing with a cup of coffee in an atmosphere of pleasant conversation. There is a *kvinne-gruppe* in almost every district.

Women's groups are not restricted to the kvinnegruppe. The husmorlag ("HEWS-moor-lahg") is a neighborhood group of women who do projects of common interest: running preschool centers, helping the elderly, doing charity work, learning a language. Notices of their activities are posted in community centers, churches, and neighborhood stores.

A *barnehage* ("BAR–neh-HAH-guh") is a kindergarten for children aged 4–7. It teaches counting, singing, crafts, socializing skills, and discipline. The *førskole* ("FEWR-skool-uh"), a special preschool for children aged 6, prepares them for entry into a Norwegian school at age 7.

EDUCATION

As education is free up to university level, nearly everyone in Norway can read and write. Children in Norway begin school at age 7, and basic education lasts nine years. Children go through six years of elementary school, followed by three years of junior high school. In order to ensure that all Norwegian children have equal educational opportunities, the Norwegian school system decides on one elementary curriculum and one method of teaching for the entire country. The curriculum focuses on nature study, physical education, social studies, and Christianity in addition to math, science, Norwegian, and foreign languages.

After junior high, many students continue on to three years of high school. This could be at a gymnasium, which focuses on general education in preparation for a course of study at a university, or vocational training in preparation for an occupation.

Norway has four universities, in Oslo, Trondheim, Bergen, and Tromsø, and several colleges, all funded by the state.

Students on the grounds of the University of Oslo. This is Norway's oldest university, founded in 1811, and the largest in terms of number of students, staff, and study programs offered.

THE COMMISSIONER FOR CHILDREN

Parliamentary debate in the 1970s on how the country could best address children's needs in a democracy where children have no vote resulted in the creation of the children's ombudsman, the Commissioner for Children.

The ombudsman's duties are to promote the interests of children and to monitor the conditions under which children grow up. The ombudsman comes under the Ministry for Children and Family Affairs. The work is twofold: gathering information from all levels of society and then approaching the authorities with problems, criticisms, and proposals for change.

The ombudsman has a high public profile as the children's spokesperson on issues important to them. On a radio and television show, the ombudsman reads out the latest cases handled and letters received from children about issues as diverse as dangerous play areas and living in families with alcoholics.

Klar Melding *("klahr MEHL-ding"), or clear message, is a toll-free hotline to the ombudsman's office for all Norwegians under 18 to ask any question or present any problem. These questions are then answered on a radio and television show.*

71

HOUSES AND GARDENS

These well-preserved houses built for German merchants of the Hanseatic League are now historical sites. Modern homes are usually located in the suburbs.

Many Norwegians living in cities join a housing cooperative called *borettslag* ("BOOR-ehts-lahg"), which finances housing projects. Single residences or apartments are then rented to its members, who pay a deposit to join in addition to the monthly rent. It's a first-come-first-served system, and some Norwegian parents sponsor their children's membership in a *borettslag* years before it is needed to give them an early start in the

line. A member who wishes to leave such a cooperative sells his or her share in it. A board of the cooperative must approve the sale—in this as well as other respects, the housing cooperative is like an exclusive club.

Attached row houses and apartments in condominiums are popular in urban areas, and single houses are usual in the country. Singles prefer one-room apartments, or *hybel* ("HEE-behl"), in private houses or apartment blocks. Summer homes near the sea or in the mountains are popular with urban Norwegians. These are usually simple shacks with a garden, where the family enjoys outdoor meals in fine weather.

Norwegians have a reputation for being self-sufficient, particularly when the work is in their own house or garden. Tasks such as painting, wallpapering, or fixing the roof are tackled with relish.

Gardening is seen as a way to commune with the soil. Most cities have a local gardening association and plant nurseries that give seasonal planting advice. In Oslo, an area is set aside for those who wish to indulge in summer gardening.

Simple houses in Lofoten are used in the summer by fishing enthusiasts and all year by the people involved in the fishing industry.

73

RELIGION

OVER 95% OF NORWEGIANS are Christian, and of these, the majority are members of the Church of Norway, which is Evangelical Lutheran. Norway's constitution guarantees complete religious freedom.

THE CHURCH OF NORWAY

The origins of the Lutheran Church go back to Martin Luther (1483–1546), a German Catholic priest who objected to some Catholic practices and started the revolution known as the Protestant Reformation. Through his actions and writings, Luther ushered in not only Protestantism, but also conditions for a revolution in economic, political, and social thought.

Opposite: The simple, pure lines of a white church in Sortland, Vesterålen.

Left: **Nidaros Cathedral in Trondheim, a city founded a thousand years ago, is a historical site.**

By the mid-16th century, most of northern Europe was Lutheran. Lutheranism reached Denmark as early as the 1520s, but it was not until 1539 that the Danish Church was established with the king as the head and the clergy as leaders in matters of faith. As it was part of the Kalmar Union with Denmark and Sweden at the time, Norway followed suit.

Lutherans, like other Protestant denominations, believe in the divinity and humanity of Jesus Christ and in the Trinity of God. They have two sacraments—baptism and the Lord's Supper. The congregation is led by either a pastor or a lay person, who is elected from the membership of a council made up of a congregation's clergy and elected lay persons.

The Church of Norway is state funded, and the government appoints pastors and church officials. In 1956, the Storting passed a law allowing women to become pastors; the state named the first female pastor in 1961.

The majority of Norwegian Lutherans are baptized, confirmed, married, and buried in religious ceremonies, but fewer than 20% of Norwegian adults attend church more than five times a year.

OLD NORSE GODS

The mythology of northern Europe goes back long before the Vikings. Viking poets and storytellers told many tales, often with conflicting details, about the gods and goddesses who lived in a heavenly place called Asgard.

Chief among the gods were Odin (or Woden), god of war and wisdom; Thor, the god of thunder and storms and slayer of trolls and giants; Frey, god of fertility and peace; Tyr, the bravest fighter among them all; and Freya, earth goddess and patron of pleasure.

Odin was the god of poetry and magic as well as war, and the early kings of Norway were fond of tracing their ancestry back to him. Odin sent women called Valkyries to lead warriors who fell in battle to the Viking heaven, Valhalla. This was a hall with 640 doors, each so wide that 960 *einherjer* ("EIN-hair-yair"), meaning the chosen ones who were admitted to Valhalla, could pass through them side by side.

Odin, who had sacrificed one of his eyes in exchange for a drink from the Well of Knowledge, had two ravens, Hugin and Mugin, as companions. The birds set out each dawn to fly over all the world and returned every night to report on all that had happened during the day. Odin's wife Frigg, the mother goddess, spun gold thread that was woven into summer clouds on her spinningwheel.

Although Odin was the chief god, Thor was more popular because of his power over the weather. His symbol was the hammer, with which he made the noise of thunder. Frey, the god of fertility and harvest, had to be appeased by Vikings. When they sowed their crops, they scattered bread and poured wine on the ground to please Frey.

Bronze image of Thor and his hammer. Many Vikings wore hammer pendants around their necks and took the name Thor as part of their own, such as Thorfnn or Thorvald. English names for some of the days of the week derive from Old Norse gods: Odin (or Woden) yields Wednesday, Thor Thursday, and Frey Friday.

NORWAY'S CONVERSION TO CHRISTIANITY

Viking sagas give an account of a feast, known as the "blood offering," where the people wanted Haakon to eat horseflesh and drink the blood in which the flesh was cooked. Haakon refused but compromised by opening his mouth over the steam. This did not satisfy the people, however, and at the next sacrifice, he was required to eat some horse liver.

During their expeditions overseas, the Vikings came in contact with Christian Europe. Some Vikings pretended to convert in order to get trade benefits, but those who settled abroad usually became Christians. Norway, however, remained faithful to the old gods. Converting the country to Christianity took 200 years and was marked by much bloodshed.

THE MISSIONARY KING Before his death, Harald Fairhair bequeathed the realm to his son Erik Bloodaxe (ruled c. 930–945). When Erik was forced from the throne, Harald's younger son, Haakon (ruled c. 945–960), who was only 15, returned to Norway and united most of the country.

Haakon, who had been educated as a Christian at the court of King Athelstan in England, was Norway's first Christian king, and he wanted Norway to become a Christian country. Although he was so well liked that he was called "Haakon the Good," he made hardly any headway in establishing Christianity. Instead, the people insisted that he participate in their old rituals.

OLAV TRYGGVASON The grandson of Harald Fairhair, Olav Tryggvason, claimed the throne of Norway in 995. As a child, he had to flee to Russia with his mother. From there he began a career as a Viking at an early age, conducting raids from the Baltics to the British Isles. Olav was so famous that he was able to collect large fleets of ships for his part in Viking attacks against England in the 980s and 990s. It was in England that he accepted Christianity and was confirmed by the Bishop of Winchester under the sponsorship of King Æthelred the Unræd—whom he had recently attacked. When he arrived in Norway in 995, Olav was immediately accepted as king in Trøndelag, and gradually by the rest of the country.

Norway's Conversion to Christianity

Aided by English missionaries, Olav was determined to bring Christianity to the people of Norway. Around the year 1000, he sent a Catholic priest with Viking Leif Eriksson to Greenland to convert the settlers. Many of the settlers converted, but for Olav in Norway, conversion was a struggle. Many still believed in the old gods, and Olav resorted to force. Using the methods of a Viking raider, Olav sailed along the coast demanding that the *tings* ("tings," or assemblies) submit and accept baptism. Those who refused were tortured or put to death. He forbade the worship of the old gods, destroyed their temples, and built the first church in Norway in a little village called Moster, south of Bergen. Olav's methods gained him many enemies. At the Battle of Svold in 1000, Olav was defeated.

NORWAY'S ETERNAL KING Olav Haraldsson landed in Norway with two shiploads of fighting men in 1015. Within a year, he had defeated Olav Tryggvasson's enemies and had himself proclaimed king of Norway. He extended his rule into parts of east Norway, which until then had been under local chieftains, and fought the Danes in the Vik area in the Oslofjord. By 1020, Olav ruled all of Norway as King Olav II.

Olav II set out to convert Norway, by force if necessary. In this last struggle between the old faith and the new, Christianity finally won. If the farmers refused to accept Christianity at a *ting*, Olav forced them to change their minds through violence, murder, and fire.

Like Olav I, Olav II's methods won him enemies. The former chieftains, backed by the king of Denmark, attacked Olav II in 1028. Olav fled to Russia but returned to try and win back his kingdom. Finally, the opposing forces met in 1030 at a farm called Stiklestad near Trondheim. Outnumbered two to one, Olav was killed and his followers defeated. His body was secretly carried to the city of Trondheim and buried in the sandbank of the River Nid. The Danish king then sent his younger son to rule Norway.

According to a legend, Olav Haraldsson was waiting in Spain for favorable winds to take him through the Straits of Gibraltar when he dreamed that a man approached him and said, "Return to your home, for you are to be king of Norway for time immemorial." On his way home, Olav spent the winter in Normandy, France, and there was converted to Christianity.

PATRON SAINT OF NORWAY

After the death of Olav II, people began to recall that there had been wondrous signs during the Battle of Stiklestad, and reports of miracles occurring at Olav's grave began to spread.

One year after the battle, Olav was declared a saint. Now Norway had its own patron saint, solidifying its ties with the rest of Europe. Olav was acknowledged as a saint throughout Europe and as far away as Constantinople. Churches were built in his honor by the hundreds, not only in Norway but in Rome and London, where there were at least six built in his name. The day of his death, July 29, became a great religious festival in the north of Europe. Even today, the date is celebrated in Trondheim with reenactments of the battle and other medieval scenes.

Olav Haraldsson began his Viking career when he was 12 years old. He fought in the Baltics, in western Europe, and in England, where in 1009 he attacked London and helped to tear down London Bridge with grappling irons. This event is remembered in the nursery rhyme, "London Bridge is Falling Down."

Saint Olav had become both a Christian martyr and a champion of national liberty. Down through the ages, his memory lived on as the symbol of a united, independent Norway. He had become the "Eternal King of Norway."

Within five years of his death, two of Olav's former enemies traveled to Russia and brought back his 11-year-old son Magnus to be king. The foreign rulers fled the country.

After the death of St. Olav, Christianity came to be accepted as the religion of the country. The old communal beer feasts were incorporated into the observance of holy days. The beer was now blessed and the first cup drunk "in honor of Christ and the Blessed Virgin for good years and peace." However, traces of the old beliefs were slow to disappear. Some types of nature and ancestor worship lingered on for centuries, and there was no serious attempt to convert the Sami until the 16th century.

OTHER CHRISTIAN CHURCHES

Besides the Lutheran Church, several other denominations have adherents in Norway. These include the Pentecostalists, Lutheran Free Church members, Methodists, Baptists, Catholics, and Jehovah's Witnesses. Many of these denominations were imported from other European countries.

The Pentecostal movement gained prominence in the early 20th century in the United States and spread rapidly to all parts of the world. Pentecostal services are enthusiastic and rousing, with an emphasis on music and congregational participation. The Pentecostal movement is attractive to people interested in social reform.

OTHER RELIGIONS

Due to the large influx of immigrants into Norway escaping political instability or economic hardship, other religions, including Islam, Judaism, Buddhism, and Hinduism, are also represented in small numbers.

A Sami congregation in a church in Kautokeino. The majority of Sami are members of the Church of Normay.

LANGUAGE

NORWEGIAN IS PART of the Germanic family of languages and draws from many European sources. As mountains and fjords historically isolated Norwegian settlements from one another, numerous dialects exist in Norway. The different dialects are very similar, and most Norwegians can understand each other, regardless of what dialect they speak.

The Sami have their own language, part of the Finno-Ugric language family. There are three major Sami dialects in the world, two of which, North Sami and South Sami, are spoken in Norway.

There are about 12,000 Norwegian Finns in Norway, who are Finnish speakers. Finnish is also part of the Finno-Ugric family of languages and is therefore distantly related to the Sami language. Finnish speakers in Norway are mostly bilingual in Finnish and Norwegian.

NORWEGIAN

Norwegian and English are related languages because both evolved from a common North Germanic language. English, German, Dutch, and Frisian split off long ago, leaving Common Scandinavian, which was spoken from about A.D. 550 to 1050. Common Scandinavian was the parent language of six official, literary languages in Scandinavia—including Danish, Bokmål ("BOOK-mawl," book Norwegian or Dano-Norwegian), Nynorsk ("NEE-noshk," new Norwegian), Swedish, Faroese, and Icelandic—plus a great variety of spoken dialects. Norwegian became a written language in the early 12th century, when the Latin alphabet was introduced.

Norwegian and English are related, but visitors to the popular resort of Geilo (*opposite*) are given directions mostly in English. And thanks to the excellent signs for *henne* ("HEN-nuh") and *ham* ("hahm"—commonly spelt *han* today) at the scent shop (*below*), they will also easily conclude that gifts can be found there for both men and women.

Two forms of the Norwegian language, Bokmål and Nynorsk, are officially used. Bokmål developed during Norway's 400-year union with Denmark and is spoken in large towns, which were strongly influenced by Danish rule. Spoken Bokmål sounds very different from Danish, but the written form is nearly identical to Danish. Created in reaction to Danish rule, Nynorsk dates from the mid-1800s. It combines elements from major rural dialects to produce a more distinctly Norwegian language.

In the 20th century, Norwegian language experts sought to streamline the two official languages into one, called Samnorsk ("SAHM-noshk," common Norwegian). The combined form was intended to simplify communication between urban and rural areas and in the mass media, which now alternate between the two forms. Some Norwegians, however, feel strongly that Bokmål and Nynorsk—as well as the many dialects that influenced them—are part of the Norwegian heritage and should not be allowed to vanish. Since 1925, all government officials have been required to answer letters in the language in which they are written, so that all bureaucrats must be competent in both forms. Local school boards decide which form will be used in elementary school, and the current split is about 20% Nynorsk and 80% Bokmål.

The language question has been a political and economic issue for at least 150 years in Norway.

BOKMÅL VS. NYNORSK

With the many influences on Norwegian throughout the centuries, two approaches to creating a modern Norwegian language have developed. One model, Nynorsk, sought to build a language as close as possible to what Norwegian might be had it not been under Danish domination for centuries. Ivar Aasen (1813–1869), a linguist and poet, analyzed western Norwegian dialects and formulated a written form for Nynorsk in *Norsk Grammatik* (Norwegian Grammar, 1864), and in *Norse Ordborg* (Norwegian Dictionary, 1873). Since Aasen drew on rural dialects, Nynorsk has great strength in poetic and literary terms describing nature and personal matters. Nynorsk is not the native language of any Norwegian speaker, and it never became the first language of Norway, but it has long had a group of supporters who associate it with a more democratic national consciousness and see Bokmål as a form of Danish.

Bokmål, earlier called Riksmål ("RIKS-mawl," language of the kingdom), used Danish as the base and Norwegianized it through changes in spelling, vocabulary, and pronunciation. Bokmål built on the speech and writings of the educated urban population. In 1856, Knud Knudsen (1812–1895), a linguist and educator, advocated a step-by-step Norwegianization of Danish spelling, a policy followed by such leading writers of the time as Henrik Ibsen. Over the years, Bokmål has retained much of the Danish vocabulary, while accepting some of the Norwegian pronunciation. Bokmål is the language taught abroad as Norwegian today.

After spelling reforms in 1907, 1917, 1938, and 1959, intended to bring the two languages closer, some hoped for the merger of the two languages into Samnorsk. Students reacted in 1960 by burning books translated into Samnorsk. Samnorsk was never accepted, and today Bokmål and Nynorsk exist side by side.

RUNES

Runes are angular letters that make up the ancient runic alphabet, one of the earliest forms of Germanic writing. Every rune had a special name, and these names are known through the oral traditions recorded in Anglo-Saxon manuscripts. The 24 runes of the early runic alphabet were divided into three groups of eight runes each. Each group was called an *ætt* ("eht") in Scandinavia, which is thought to mean a group of eight. Later, the runes were called *futhark* ("FEW-thahrk"), which is the word spelt by the first six letters.

RUNIC WRITING

The oldest written examples of any Germanic languages are the runic inscriptions in Scandinavia. About 3,500 runic inscriptions have been found, on objects as diverse as weapons, spear blades, and brooches. The most enduring examples have been the runestones.

Runestones are solid stone slabs carved with runic inscriptions and ornamental designs. The earliest known stone dates back to A.D. 300. Very little is known about the origin of runestones, but experts believe they were linked to magic and sorcery, and perhaps religious rituals. It is thought that the common material for runic inscriptions was wood, but none has survived. Surviving runestones show two runic alphabets: the older, used from the third to the ninth centuries, had 24 letters, and the later had only 16 letters, a simplification of the earlier alphabet.

Runic inscriptions were often set within a decorated snake or dragon coil. Occasionally, other ornamental designs were used as well. Stone engravers sometimes took it upon themselves to include additional information to the commissioned text. Much of our information about the political, economic, and cultural conditions of those times comes from these runestones. The stones also tell of Viking journeys as far away as Byzantium and Baghdad, as many were memorials to someone who died on the journeys. It is from the pictures on these stones that we know of Old Norse legends of Sigurd the dragon slayer and Thor the thunder god.

THE SAMI LANGUAGE

The Sami language is not Germanic, as Norwegian is, but is part of the Finno-Ugric language family, which is related to Finnish and Hungarian. Sami speakers are divided into three main dialect groups: North Sami, mostly spoken in northern Norway, Finland, and Sweden; East Sami, which includes Inari and Skolt in Eastern Finland and Kola Sami from the Kola Peninsula; and the least common, South Sami, still represented by a few scattered speakers from central Norway to north-central Sweden. Each of these dialect groups has various subgroups. Sami dialects are so different from one another that a member of one dialect group cannot understand a member of another. When Norwegian Sami of different dialect groups meet, they communicate in Norwegian.

North Sami has a literary tradition that began with the 17th century Swedish Sami Bible and other religious translations; in the mid-20th century, elementary schools that used Sami as the language of instruction were found in many larger North Sami communities. The Sami in Norway use a special system of writing that was created to accommodate a wide range of variations in dialect.

The vocabulary of the Sami does not include words for war, farming, or things unfamiliar to them. When it comes to nature, they are not lacking: eight seasons exist in their vocabulary and 90 variations of snow conditions.

This Sami woman from Finnmark is likely to speak Norwegian in addition to her Sami dialect.

ARTS

NORWAY HAS A LONG TRADITION in the arts—descending from the poems and legends of Viking times, through Danish influence during Danish rule, to the nationalist concerns of modern times. Among the oldest artistic works in Norway are the intricate wood carvings with which the Vikings decorated ships, buildings, wagons, sleighs, swords, and other objects.

SCULPTURE

The first Norwegian sculptor to win international fame, Gustav Vigeland (1869–1943), has an entire park in Oslo dedicated to him. Vigeland Museum, which holds Vigeland's ashes and many of his works, is also located in Vigeland Park. In the 1920s, the municipality of Oslo offered Vigeland this building for his studio and residence. In return he donated all his works to the city.

Vigeland Park was designed by Vigeland himself. The park exhibits many of his best works, whose main theme is the various phases of human life, from infancy to old age. Many of his sculptures represent scenes from everyday life. In *Angry Boy*, Vigeland immortalized a young boy throwing a tantrum. The work that most people see as the park's main masterpiece is *The Monolith*, a sculpture 55 feet (17 meters) tall, representing 121 humans struggling toward a summit. Vigeland Park, which also features a sculpted self-portrait of Vigeland, draws about one million visitors a year.

Above and opposite: **Angry Boy** and **Delicate Mother and Child**, two sculptures in Vigeland Park. Vigeland's work is said to be influenced by the French sculptor Auguste Rodin and by English and French Gothic sculpture.

PAINTING

The nationalistic movement in literature that arose in the 19th century influenced the visual arts. Paintings of Norwegian landscapes and scenes of daily life replaced visual arts with Christian and Viking themes. Johan Christian Dahl (1788–1857) was at the forefront of the development of a Norwegian style of painting. Dahl also introduced the mountain as a symbol that would recur in the works of later artists and writers. He taught in Dresden, Germany.

Ladies on the Quay departs from the themes of death and despair that characterize many paintings by Edvard Munch.

EDVARD MUNCH Norway's best-known artist is Edvard Munch (1863–1944). Munch's ability to portray the trauma of modern psychic life through distortion of colors and forms made him one of the most influential modern artists.

Munch, who came from an old Norwegian professional family, was greatly affected by the deaths of his mother when he was 5 and his eldest sister when he was 14. Many critics feel that Munch's childhood explains the melancholy in his paintings. Munch himself said, in 1889, "No one should paint interiors anymore, people reading and women knitting. They should be living people who breathe and feel, suffer and love." His better-known works include *The Sick Child, Ashes, Death in the Room, Jealousy,* and *Summer Night.*

Munch gave his works to the city of Oslo, where they are now housed at the Munch Museum. In 1994, his best-known painting, *Skrik* or *The Scream,* which he called a scream against nature, was stolen.

MUSIC

Norway has a long tradition of music that includes folk songs, fiddling, and brass bands. Just about every school has a marching band, which is where many of Norway's jazz musicians got their start.

Norway's most famous composer is Edvard Grieg (1843–1907). Grieg did not write symphonies but took on large projects. He is world famous for writing the music for Henrik Ibsen's *Peer Gynt.* He is also known for his piano sonatas, 10 volumes of lyrical pieces inspired by the poems of Henrik Ibsen and Arne Garborg. Grieg, who has written Norwegian folk songs and music for Norwegian dances, is equally well known in Norway for a little rubber frog that he kept in his pocket. It is believed that by rubbing its rough-textured back before a concert he calmed his nerves. The frog is part of the permanent Grieg exhibit at the composer's home.

Modern composer Arne Nordheim (b. 1931) took Norwegian classical music by storm two generations after Grieg's death. He produces experimental works, often combining orchestral music with taped electronically processed acoustic sounds.

Edvard Grieg's compositions were stamped with the mark of his Norwegian heritage.

When Knut Hamsun visited the United States in 1886, he worked in the fields in North Dakota and as a streetcar conductor in Chicago. He also gave lectures on modern European writers in Minneapolis.

LITERATURE

Norwegian Vikings who settled in Iceland passed on their beliefs, history, and myths through stories. These were written down in the 13th century *Eddas*, books that tell of the mythical gods and heroes of Scandinavia.

The first important writer of the modern period was Henrik Wergeland (1808–1845). He wrote love and nature poems and numerous essays. He established a free personal lending library. A devout nationalist, Wergeland called upon Norwegians to free themselves of Danish influence and set up a school in his own home where he taught Norwegian. He set the pattern for creative writers to be public advocates for democracy and freedom.

Wergeland's sister Camilla Collett (1813–1895) wrote Norway's first feminist novel, *The Governor's Daughter*, in 1855, decrying the position of women forced into marriage. Collett inspired other women writers, including Amalie Skram (1847–1905), who in her novels *Constance Ring* and *Betrayed*, continued Collett's theme of disastrous marriages.

Around the turn of the 20th century, Norwegian writers focused on the struggles of the individual. Many 20th century novels explore social problems and feature protagonists who reject modern society. In 1920, Knut Hamsun (1859–1952), best known for his novels *Hunger* and *Growth of the Sun*, was awarded the Nobel Prize in literature.

HENRIK IBSEN

The work of Henrik Ibsen (1828–1906) revolutionized theater. His plays aroused enormous criticism, but people flocked to see them. James Joyce was so enamored of Ibsen's plays that he taught himself Norwegian in order to study them. A great supporter of women's rights, Ibsen is known for creating many great female characters, such as Nora in *A Doll's House*, which is about the hypocrisy of marriage and women's liberation.

Ibsen's major plays are set in Norway, with a recognizably Norwegian landscape, but his characters and themes have universal significance. Ibsen portrayed people as they are; his characters struggle with problems that society of their time was afraid to mention, such as marital discord and illegitimacy. Over the course of 50 years, Ibsen published 25 plays and a volume of poetry.

"I would rather play Ibsen than eat," declared American actress Eva Le Gallienne (1899–1991), who translated and acted in many of Ibsen's plays.

SIGRID UNDSET, NOBEL LAUREATE

In 1928, another Norwegian writer, Sigrid Undset (1882–1949), was awarded the Nobel Prize in literature for her long historical novel *Kristin Lavransdatter*, set in 13th century Norway. Undset, considered to be Norway's greatest woman writer, was taught the Old Norse sagas and Scandinavian folk songs at an early age by her archeologist father. Although Undset is not regarded as a feminist, her novels provide an insight into women's lives not found elsewhere in Norwegian fiction. Her early novels centered on the lives of ordinary working women and how they dealt with the conflict between personal needs and ambitions and family responsibilities.

During the 1930s, Undset wrote vehemently against the rise of Nazism in Germany, which put her on the Nazis' wanted list. When the Nazis occupied Norway, Undset escaped to Sweden, then across Siberia to Japan and then to the United States. She spent the war years actively working for the Norwegian government in exile. After the war, she returned to her home in Lillehammer and died four years later.

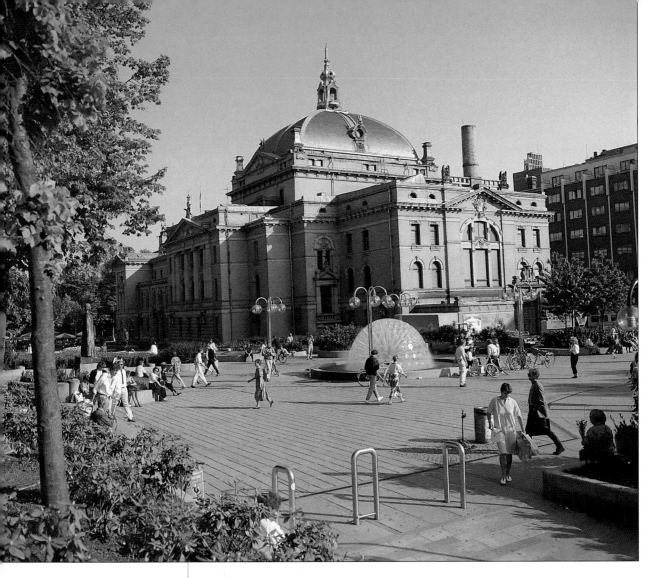

DRAMA

The National Theater in Oslo was opened in 1899. In the late 1960s, the theaters in Oslo, Bergen, Stavanger, and Trondheim underwent an expansion and started subsidiary theaters. This doubled the production of plays and helped the boom in drama and the performing arts that Norway has experienced since the late 1970s.

By European standards, Norway's theater traditions are very young. Professional theater began only in 1827, when Swede Johan Peter Strømberg opened his theater in Oslo. Norway's oldest existing theater is the National Stage in Bergen, which was opened in 1876.

Henrik Ibsen, Norway's most famous playwright, well known all over the world for plays such as *Peer Gynt* and *A Doll's House*, is acknowledged as the father of modern Norwegian drama. Norway also had another prominent playwright, Nordahl Grieg, who wrote plays that dealt with the human psyche and questioned one's inner self.

The National Traveling Theater, or *Riksteatret* ("riks-teh-AH-ter-eht"), was founded in 1948, using the Swedish *Riksteatret* as its model. The *Riksteatret* brings professional drama to towns and villages that would otherwise be deprived, being too small to support their own theater companies. It is the equivalent of the circus coming to town, and no one who can help it will miss a performance of the *Riksteatret*.

Permanent theaters are awarded grants that cover almost 90% of their operating expenses by government, county, and local authorities.

MOVIES

Most Norwegian movie theaters show foreign films, mainly from the United States and Europe. The Norwegian movie industry is still in its early stages, although it is starting to make a name for itself. Some Norwegian movies have traveled the Atlantic, such as Arne Schouen's *Gategutter* (Street Boys) and *Ni Liv* (Nine Lives), which was nominated for an Academy Award in 1957.

The early 1980s saw the Norwegian movie industry dominated by women directors like Vibeke Løkkeberg, Anja Breien, and Bente Erichsen, but in the late 1980s, male directors caught up with successful action movies. In 1986, Oddvar Einarson's movie *X* was awarded the judges' special prize in the Venice film festival.

Perhaps the best-known Norwegian movie is Nils Gaup's *Veiviseren* (Pathfinder), which was nominated for an Academy Award for Best Foreign Film. *Veiviseren* is based on Sami folklore from the Middle Ages. It was a great international success. Nils Gaup produced another successful movie in 1991: there are Norwegian and English versions of his *Haakon Haakonsen*, which had mass appeal because of its shipwreck and adventure theme.

In the big cities, watching a movie is a regular affair. However, many of the smaller towns do not have a movie theater. For residents of these towns, going to watch a movie is a real night out, as they have to drive to the nearest large town or city. Often they will get together with a couple of friends, have dinner first, and then make their way to the town in time for the movie.

SAMI ARTISTIC TRADITIONS

FOLK DRESS The only district where folk dress is still worn daily as well as for holidays is Lappland. In the winter, the Sami who inhabit Lappland wear fur from head to foot, but in the summer, they wear their most colorful traditional clothes. Their dress has fabric around the throat and shoulders patterned with delicate embroidery. Samis often wear beautiful belts woven in bright colors, such as the ones at right.

THE *JOIK* An old Sami form of musical expression is the *joik* ("yoy-IK"), a type of yodeling. Traditionally, the *joik* imitates animals, such as the wolf, reindeer, or long-tailed duck. A *joik* can also tell an ancient Sami myth or be a commentary on current events. The most popular form of *joik* are character sketches of individuals that can be changed as the person changes. A Sami does not write his or her own *joik*, and once one is written about a person, it is customary to regard it as belonging to that person. The memory of deceased persons is kept alive by reciting their *joik*.

In traditional religious ceremonies, the *joik* was used to help the shaman enter a trance while beating a drum. During the Norwegianization process, the *joik* and drumming were outlawed. Today, Sami revivalization has evoked a renewed interest in the *joik* tradition, and it has acquired value as an important cultural symbol. In recent years, one *joik* made it to the top of the Norwegian hit parade.

STAVKIRKER *ARCHITECTURE*

Norway's rich tradition in wood carving is documented in stories of the medieval period, when carpentry was a craft entrusted only to men of rank. When Norway was converted to Christianity, Norwegians developed their own form of religious architecture in the *Stavkirker* ("stahv-KHEER-ker"), or stave churches, which are thought to be quintessentially Norwegian. Norway had over 900 stave churches in the medieval period. Only 30 remain intact. No nails were used in the construction of stave churches.

Early stave churches retained Viking decorative elements and also displayed Christian influences from other parts of Europe. These churches were small, dark, and plain, without pews or pulpits. Animals and intertwining decorative lines, similar to Viking wood carvings, decorated the doors, especially the large west doors that served as the main entrance.

Opposite: **The Borgund stave church in Sogn. Dragon heads, a Viking symbol, as well as Christian crosses, are common features of stave churches.**

LEISURE

SKIING IS a Norwegian passion, a natural consequence of the climate and terrain of the country. Skiing is not a recent invention. A 4,000-year-old rock carving in Nordland near the Arctic Circle shows a person on two skis. Skis about 2,300 years old have been found preserved in bogs. Old Norse mythology had both a ski god (Ull) and a ski goddess (Skade).

Soccer is also popular in Norway, as it is in most other parts of the world. Also popular are boating, fishing, rowing, swimming, and cycling.

A NATION OF SKIERS

Almost every Norwegian owns a pair of skis. Norwegians take their first skiing lessons at age 2 or 3. Schoolchildren look forward to ski days and ski vacations, and adults often go off on ski runs to unwind after a hard day at work. After dusk, adults ski the many miles of lighted trails through woods wearing a cap with a light, similar to a miner's cap. Those feeling deprived during the summer often pack their skis and make their way to the glaciers of the Jotunheimen National Park.

There is a saying that Norwegians are born with skis on their feet. Certainly, they are taught to ski at a very early age.

Opposite: **Norwegian children are conscientious about using a helmet when riding a bicycle.**

Norway is known as the home of modern skiing. Sondre Norheim (1825–1897), a poor farmer from Morgedal in the Telemark region, devised a ski that was narrower in the middle and had stiff bindings around the heel. This was called the Telemark ski, and it enabled Norheim to execute jumps and turn without losing his skis, earning him the title "father of modern skiing."

Norwegians excel at speed skating, and their athletes carry away prizes at every Winter Olympics. Here, Norwegian silver medallist Kjell Storlid goes through his paces at Lillehammer in 1994.

Norheim and some ski enthusiasts soon became known for their daring feats and traveled to competitions where they would demonstrate their techniques. Norheim was 50 when he retired from competitions, but he taught his techniques to children. Later, he went to the United States, where others from Telemark had introduced skiing.

The first recorded skiing competitions with prizes in Norway date from 1866. By 1903, foreigners were taking part in the annual competitions. With the popularity of skiing as a sport instead of simply for transportation, hotels that previously closed for the winter discovered they could now stay open all year round. In 1924, the first Winter Olympics were held in Chamonix in France, with Norwegians taking the top four spots in the 31-mile (50-kilometer) race.

ICE SKATING

The first speed-skating contest in Norway was held on the fjord near Oslo's Akershus Fortress in 1885. In the 1950s, speed-skating champions were national heroes. Since then, interest in the sport has diminished, although in 1991, Norway gained a new national hero in Johan Koss, who made sports history when he broke three world records during the world speed skating championships in the Netherlands, followed by winning a gold medal at the 1994 Winter Olympics.

In figure-skating, Sonja Henie, Norway's darling of the 1920s, brought fame to Norway as the world's figure-skating champion at 13. She retained the title for 10 years and won an Olympic gold medal three times.

WOMEN IN SPORTS

Although Norwegian women today are winning many of the top spots in international sporting events such as marathons, handball, and soccer, it has been only recently that women athletes were fully accepted in Norway. In 1888, Lillehammer sponsored the world's first ski races for women, but Norwegian men were critical of women skiers who dared to drink a mug of beer or stretch their legs by a fireplace after skiing. It is only since the 1960s that Norwegian women have been taken seriously in cross-country skiing competitions.

The acceptance of sportswomen in Norway is attributed to Grete Waitz (b. 1953), who won the New York marathon nine times out of 10 between 1978 and 1988. She started a run through the streets of Oslo in 1982, and it has become an annual event.

In 1927, at the World Figure-Skating Championship in Oslo, Sonja Henie (*above*) took first place, beating Hanna Planck-Szabo of Austria. The decision was mired in controversy, however, because all three Norwegian judges voted for Henie, whereas the Austrian and German judges gave higher marks to Planck-Szabo. After this, no country has had more than one judge on the panel.

SPORTS FOR THE PHYSICALLY CHALLENGED

In 1964, Erling Stordahl, who is blind, arranged the first ski race for the visually handicapped, using deeper ski trails and a guiding system of beeping sounds along the trail. His idea was picked up by many others, and today disabled athletes can participate in 17 different sports organized by the Norwegian Sports Organization for the Disabled, founded in 1971.

NO FENCES

Norway's grand and beautiful wilderness areas, which have inspired artists and musicians, are accessible to everyone in Norway. Norwegians spend much of their free time hiking, skiing, fishing, cycling, and mountain climbing. In fact, the reluctance of Oslo residents to leave the city, which lies in the middle of the Nordmarka forest area, because they are so fond of walks through the woods is referred to as the Nordmarka syndrome. To help trekkers, the Norwegian Mountain Touring Association, the oldest organization of its kind in the world, marks trails and runs cabins for overnight accommodation.

The right of access to uncultivated areas is very important in Norway. Fortunately, along with free access, most Norwegians are conscious of their obligations. They know they may not walk about in newly planted forest; break off, cut, or in any way damage plants; disturb animals and birds, including their nests and young; or trample fields and meadows.

INKY Norwegian children are encouraged to enjoy the outdoors from a very early age. Along with a love for the outdoors, they are very conscious of environmental issues. When she was a child, Norwegian Bente Roestad saw an octopus for the first time while vacationing in Greece. Years later, she created stories about the octopus, whom she called Inky, for her 5-year-old nephew. The simple stories about the wise blue octopus grew into a series of books and later a television series about the threat of pollution to marine life. The shows provoked 40,000 calls from children who wanted to know how they could help, and the Norwegian Society for the Conservation of Nature started the Inky Club for children aged 5–13. Its members call in to radio shows, expose environmental misdemeanors, and write articles for newspapers. One environmental "detective," Bjørn Carlsen, aged 13, discovered that industrial waste was seeping from a landfill into a children's play area and also polluting a nearby lake.

Long-distance cyclists take the precaution of wearing helmets in case of spills.

Opposite, top: **A family goes mountain hiking in Telemark.**

Opposite, bottom: **Not too many boys this size can claim they have caught pike so big.**

EXPLORERS

Harking back to the traditional occupation of their Viking ancestors as daring explorers who set sail for parts unknown, several Norwegians have attempted grueling expeditions to far reaches of the Earth. They include Fridtjof Nansen, Otto Sverdrup, Roald Amundsen, Thor Heyerdahl, Ragnar Thorseth, and most recently, Liv Arnesen.

FRIDTJOF NANSEN To prove his hypothesis that the Arctic current flowed from Siberia toward the North Pole and then down to Greenland, scientist Fridtjof Nansen designed a boat that would not break apart under the enormous pressure of ice. Together with 13 crew members, he headed east in July 1893. Off the northeast coast of Siberia, the *Fram* was frozen into the ice pack. With knowledge gained from years of study, Nansen knew the boat would not pass over the North Pole. With a companion, three light sleds, 28 dogs, three kayaks, and food for 100 days, he set out in March 1895 for the North Pole.

By early April, Nansen realized they would not make it to the North Pole, although he had gone farther than any previous explorer, and they attempted to journey to Franz Joseph Land, 400 miles (640 kilometers) to the southwest. It was August when they reached an uninhabited island north of Franz Joseph Land, and winter was closing in, so they dug a three-foot hollow, made a roof of walrus skins, and sat out the nine-month winter.

In June 1896, they made it to one of the southern islands when they encountered the English explorer Frederick Jackson, who had been commissioned to find an overland route to the North Pole. Nansen returned to Norway on Jackson's ship to a hero's welcome. A week later, the *Fram* arrived in Norway, having drifted from Siberia to Svalbard, proving Nansen's theory.

OTTO SVERDRUP The captain of the *Fram* for Nansen's drift expedition, Otto Sverdrup (1854–1930), took the *Fram* on a second expedition to the Arctic islands north of Canada and spent four years charting unexplored territory. Between 1910 and 1920, he led other polar expeditions. His maps were a valuable resource for explorers who came after him.

ROALD AMUNDSEN Like Fridtjof Nansen, Roald Amundsen (1872–1928) was a professional expeditioner who knew that courage without a lot of planning achieved little. Amundsen realized that success for an Arctic expedition meant combining the roles of scientist and navigator. In

During his first voyage, Roald Amundsen (*above*) and his crew spent a summer and two winters doing research on King William Island. From the Netsilik Inuit people, Amundsen learned patience and the value of pacing oneself. The Inuit know that sweat can kill you in the Arctic, as well as exhaust you so that you cannot expend a burst of energy in an emergency. These lessons stood Amundsen in good stead for his later expedition to the South Pole.

Liv Arnesen, a 41-year-old Norwegian, became the first woman to reach the South Pole alone when she reached it on Christmas Day in 1994 after trudging 746 miles (1,200 km) in 50 days.

preparation, he not only trained physically by playing soccer, skiing, and sleeping with the window open in the winter, but also studied navigation and the theories of magnetism.

Amundson wanted to be the first to navigate the Northwest Passage. In the previous 400 years, 50 or 60 expeditions had been launched without success. In 1903, with a crew of six, Amundsen set out to navigate the Northwest Passage in a 31-year-old small herring boat. He was convinced the smallness of his vessel and patience would get him farther than the others, who had used much larger boats.

He was right. Amundsen got through the entire Northwest Passage, including a shallow island-dotted strait never before navigated. He wrote later that "it was just like sailing through an uncleared field." If he had been in a larger boat, he would not have succeeded.

PLANTING THE NORWEGIAN FLAG AT THE SOUTH POLE

After months of preparation, Amundsen was just about to set out in Nansen's *Fram* for the North Pole when news that American Robert Peary had reached it reverberated around the world. Amundsen immediately changed his course for Antarctica and the South Pole, determined to reach it ahead of the British expedition headed by Robert Scott.

At the Bay of Whales in the Ross Sea, Amundsen set out overland with four men and 52 dogs. One of the four men was Olav Bjaaland, a skiing champion from Morgedal, who was given the task of making sure the skis and sleds were in top condition all the time. On December 14, 1911, the Norwegian group reached the South Pole and planted the Norwegian flag on King Haakon VII's Plateau. This was the expedition that made Roald Amundsen a household name around the world. Five weeks later, Robert Scott arrived at the pole to find the Norwegian flag and Amundsen's tent.

Amundsen died in 1928 while attempting to rescue Unberto Nobile, an explorer whose airship had crashed while attempting to fly over the North Pole. At a memorial service for Amundsen, who was buried in the Arctic, Fridtjof Nansen said that Amundsen had "returned to the expanses of the Arctic Ocean, where his life's work lay."

THOR HEYERDAHL Perhaps the best-known explorer of the 20th century, Thor Heyerdahl (b. 1914) did not follow in the footsteps of Nansen or Amundsen by exploring unchartered territories. Anthropology was his interest.

While a zoology and geography student, he traveled in 1937 to Polynesia to do research on animal life in the valleys of the island of Fatu-Hiva. Accepted anthropological theories posited that ancestors of the Polynesians had sailed there from Asia, but Heyerdahl noticed the people had much in common with South Americans in food, statues, and myths.

Thor Heyerdahl (*above*) sailed his reed boats under the United Nations flag with a multinational crew to show that peaceful coexistence, even under extreme conditions, is possible.

To prove wrong the scientists who argued that South Americans could not have reached Polynesia in their primitive vessels, Heyerdahl set out on his famous *Kon Tiki* expedition. In 1947, he built a raft in the style of the Incas—a log raft held together by ropes and wooden pegs—and set out from Peru with five companions. In 101 days, having covered 5,000 miles (8,045 kilometers), he reached the Raroia Atoll in Polynesia. He did not prove that the Polynesians' ancestors came from South America, but Heyerdahl proved it was possible.

Heyerdahl later made many other voyages in replicas of prehistoric boats. He traveled on papyrus reed boats, named *Ra I* and *Ra II*, from North Africa to the Caribbean in 1969 and 1970. In 1978, he sailed from the Middle East to East Asia and back to Africa in an Iraqi reed boat. All of Heyerdahl's voyages attempted to show the links between major early civilizations. Heyerdahl believes that the world's oceans served as highways for humankind since the first boats were built.

FESTIVALS

NORWAY HAS festivals of Christian origin, such as Christmas and Easter, and others of pre-Christian origin that have been converted into either Christian or secular festivals, such as Midsummer's Day. Norwegians also celebrate worldwide holidays, such as Labor Day, and festivals found nowhere else, such as their Constitution Day and *russ* ("rewss") celebrations.

Because Norwegians work hard the rest of the year, they really let their hair down and celebrate on festival days. The streets are filled with people, and in the cities and towns it looks like one big party.

Labor Day in Europe has traditionally been a day to demand better working conditions, increased benefits, and shorter working hours. However, in Norway, many feel there is little left to demand, with workers entitled to four weeks' paid vacation, two and a half days at Christmas, a minimum of five days at Easter, and the additional holidays of Ascension Day, Whitsuntide Monday, Labor Day, and Constitution Day, plus sick days for oneself or one's children and paid maternity and paternity leave. So Labor Day is enjoyed as a holiday.

Other holidays include the Holmenkollen Ski Festival, the Bergen concert and theater festival at the end of May, and an international jazz week in Molde at the end of July. Early fall brings the international Ibsen festival in Oslo, and December 10 is the day of the Nobel Peace Prize ceremony, an Oslo event that garners international attention.

> *"We use our holidays to celebrate the sun. We celebrate the arrival of the sun, the summer solstice, we journey to the mountains in search of the sun, and on the day we miss it the most, because it is farthest away, we cheer ourselves with a grand Christmas feast."*
>
> —*Thor Heyerdahl*

Opposite: **Norwegians usually wear traditional clothes only during festivals and important occasions, such as weddings. The *bunad* ("BOO-nahd") is a beautifully embroidered traditional dress, and the embroidery varies with each district. Traditional clothes are costly and handed down from parent to child.**

NORWEGIAN HOLIDAYS

January 23	Midsummer's Day	November 1	All Saints' Day
April 14	Easter	December 10	Nobel Peace Prize
May 1	Labor Day		Presentation
May 17	Constitution Day	December 25	*Jul* (Christmas)
	Children's Day	December 26	Boxing Day

CONSTITUTION DAY

Constitution Day is the Norwegian equivalent of the Fourth of July celebrations in the United States. It falls on May 17, the anniversary of the day in 1814 when Norway's elected National Assembly issued a constitution that declared an end to the 400-year union with Denmark.

Constitution Day has been celebrated in various ways over the decades. After independence in 1905, parades emphasized nationhood. During the Nazi occupation of World War II, Constitution Day celebrations were forbidden. In the decades since World War II, parades have emphasized democratic rights, freedom of the press, and constitutional government.

May 17 has also become Children's Day in Norway, and thousands of schoolchildren participate in processions with their school bands in cities, towns, and villages all over Norway. The Oslo parade ends at the Royal Palace, where the royal family waves to the children from the balcony.

The day is marked by firecrackers set off at dawn, between 4 and 5 a.m. High school graduates drive around in cars decorated with flowers and branches, wearing their *russ* or graduation suits. For them, Constitution Day marks the beginning of a three-week celebration of the end of high school.

"Now stands the flagpole bare behind Eidsvoll's budding trees. But in such an hour as this, We know what freedom is."

—Norwegian poet Nordahl Grieg, on the Nazi ban on Constitution Day celebrations

RUSS CELEBRATIONS

High school graduates celebrate their graduation in a unique style, wearing their *russ* gowns and engaging in a three-week-long celebration. The term *russ* originated from the term for university-bound graduates, who were known as *röd russer*, or red russ, because of their red graduation gowns. *Russ* students are identified by the color they choose to wear in common. It might be red for arts graduates or blue for science graduates.

Russ students are allowed many liberties. They are permitted to make as much noise as they wish, early in the morning, late at night, or all day. They can spray silly jingles about their teachers on the pavements with washable paint, or serenade teachers in the early hours of the morning. They can have as much fun as they wish, providing they do not engage in acts of vandalism that destroy property.

Teachers are not the only targets of *russ* students. Neighbors may have a rude, but never insulting, jingle about them sprayed on the pavement in front of their house. They will be embarrassed by it, but it is all permitted and accepted in a spirit of fun.

Russ graduates in high spirits on a street in Oslo. Years ago, *russ* celebrations had a cultural emphasis, with graduates organizing plays and other performances. The cultural aspect is missing today.

Opposite: **May 17 is an occasion for parades with the Norwegian flag and, for a few, for wearing their** *bunad*, **or traditional dress.**

Midsummer's Eve is the time for small barbecues near the big bonfire, with sausages, fancy dress, and much gaiety. Mindful of fire hazards, parents spray the grass nearby with water before the bonfire party.

EASTER

Easter celebrations are less a religious occasion in Norway than a rejoicing in the lengthening of the days, a sign that summer is not too far away. In the north, the Sami gather to celebrate weddings, confirmations, and baptisms, and all Norwegians who live north of the Arctic Circle celebrate the return of the sun after weeks of darkness.

Although many Norwegians spend the five-day Easter break with family and close friends, Easter also is a time for celebrating solitude and independence and communing with nature. Many Norwegians take off on solitary journeys up into the mountains to do just that. A popular Easter joke is the one about a Norwegian professor who, when asked how he had enjoyed his Easter holiday in the mountains, replied, "It was a total failure. I met somebody."

MIDSUMMER'S DAY

Midsummer, or the summer solstice, is the longest day of the year. Early Vikings often held their assemblies on Midsummer's Day, which was also allegedly the annual meeting day for witches. The feast of the bonfires on the summer solstice is one of the oldest celebrations in northern Europe. In Christian times, the day was renamed St. John's Eve, for John the Baptist. Today, heaps of wood are collected for days before. On Midsummer's Eve, huge bonfires are lit, and the crowd drinks, eats, and dances all night long.

CHRISTMAS

Jul ("yewl"), or Christmas, is a busy time for churches, which hold special advent services, and for households, as traditionally all the wood must be cut, cakes baked, food prepared, and beer brewed by December 21, St. Thomas' Day. On Christmas Eve, families sit down to a traditional Christmas dinner, which includes *pinnekjøtt* ("PINE-shuht") and *gløgg* ("gluhg"). *Pinnekjøtt*, meaning twig meat, is salted lamb ribs, so named because a rack of birch twigs is placed in the bottom of the pan used to steam the ribs. *Gløgg*, descended from the Viking drink mead, is juice mulled with raisins, ginger, cardamom, cinnamon, and other spices, served warm. It is a favorite Christmas drink. After the meal, the family walks around the Christmas tree singing traditional carols. Gifts are exchanged and opened, and the celebrations last for 20 days, until St. Knut's Day, January 13.

Norwegians decorate their Christmas trees with white candles, a remnant of traditional midwinter bonfires. An almond ring cake, which takes a long time to prepare and is therefore usually served only on festive occasions, takes pride of place at the table. In the 18th century, food was often left on the table from Christmas Eve to Epiphany (January 6). All who entered the house had to sample the food, for if they left without doing so they were thought to "carry Christmas out of the house."

THE GHOSTS OF CHRISTMAS

Before Santa Claus was imported into Norway by department stores hoping to increase sales, Christmas was a time of visits from ghosts. Norwegians believed their ancestors returned to their earthly homes in midwinter. Until the late 19th century, straw was left in many homes for the invisible "guests" to sleep on during the holiday season, and bread was left out for them to eat. In a popular fairy tale, a family was regularly chased out of their home by in invading horde of Christmas ghosts. The ghosts were finally outwitted by a white bear, and never returned.

FOOD

LIVING CLOSE TO THE SEA, Norwegians historically have depended on seafood for much of their diet. Cooks prepare fish in various ways, frequently serving it with boiled potatoes and vegetables at the main meal of the day, *middag* ("mid-DAHG"), which most people eat between 4 and 6 p.m. Norwegians eat three other meals—breakfast, lunch, and supper. Each meal features *smørbrød* ("SMUHR-brur"): open-face sandwiches of bread or crackers layered with cheese, jam, salmon spread, boiled egg, tomato, cucumber, sausage, herring, or sardines.

Some Norwegian delicacies are salty and have a strong odor. *Gravet* ("grah-VUHT"), or smoked salmon, is a favorite, and some Norwegians savor *rakørret* ("RAHK-uhr-ruht"), or trout aged for months until it has a soft, buttery consistency and a pungent odor. Mutton is the most common meat, and blood sausage—a mixture of blood and flour—is a national speciality.

Traditional desserts include fruit soups, *rømmegrøt* ("RUH-muh-gruhrt"), or sour cream porridge, and fresh berries during the summer.

Middag is the time when families sit down to eat together and share the events of their day.

Opposite: **Cabbage is a basic ingredient in salads, often taking the place of lettuce, which is more expensive in Norway.**

SMØRGÅSBORD

Smørgåsbord ("SMUR-gaws-boor"), a word that has entered the English vocabulary, means an overflowing buffet table and an opportunity to indulge oneself. *Smørgåsbord* is a Swedish word to describe the Scandinavian practice of laying out a buffet spread with a multitude of different dishes, from spicy cured herring and other fish to meats, salads, and cheeses. The

term literally means "bread and butter table," and the idea was that one helped oneself to various dishes and ate them with bread and butter. The actual Norwegian (and Danish) name is *koldt bord* ("KOLT-boor"), which means cold table, but the Swedish word is better known and generally used. A ritual is attached to the *smørgåsbord*. One must begin with the various cured herring, take a fresh plate for the meats and salads, and then finish up with cheese. The usual beverages served during a *smørgåsbord* are schnapps, *aquavit* ("AH-qeh-vit"), and beer.

TYPICAL NORWEGIAN DISHES

Almost every Norwegian dish includes potatoes—sliced, boiled, fried, in stews, and in any other way imaginable. The potato has been a staple of the Norwegian diet since the early 19th century.

Norwegians eat a heavily meat- and fish-based diet. A children's favorite is *kjøttkaker* ("shet-KAH-ker"), or meatballs in brown sauce. Norwegians have been known to take canned *kjøttkaker* with them when traveling in case they do not get accustomed to the local food. *Fårikål* ("fawr-EE-kawl") is a traditional thick, rich lamb stew cooked with cabbage. This is often made in the fall, when mutton is abundant. *Fiskeboller* ("fis-kuh-BOWL-er"), or Norwegian fishballs made from a mixture of fish, salt, and water, are an acquired taste. *Lapskaus* ("lahps-KAH-oos"), a meat and potato stew made with salted pork or leftover meats, is a thick, chunky stew popular with everyone.

Lutefisk ("LEW-tuh-fisk"), usually served a few weeks before Christmas, is most definitely an acquired taste. It is prepared by soaking cod in lye water for two or three days until the flesh is soft enough to poke a finger through. The cod is then soaked in running cold water for two days to remove all traces of lye, and then cut into large pieces and boiled or poached. *Lutefisk* is often served with *lefse* ("LEHF-suh"), or Norwegian flatbread, and can be eaten with peas or white sauce and mustard.

Finnish beef is not really beef at all, but a Sami speciality made from shaved reindeer meat browned in butter and seasoned with salt and pepper. It is often served with some goat cheese, lingonberry compote, and, of course, boiled or mashed potatoes.

MUSHROOM AND BERRY PICKING

More Norwegians are acquiring a taste for mushrooms. This increasing interest in mushrooms has developed into a pastime of nature walks combined with mushroom picking. Berry picking, on the other hand, has long been a leisure activity for the entire family. The rewards of both mushroom and berry picking include delicious dishes, jams, and pies.

Norway's vast forests are public domain, even if parts of it are owned by farmers. There is a right of public access to all forested areas in Norway, and everyone is free to pick mushrooms or berries.

The potato arrived in Norway in the 18th century and was first only available to government employees and the upper classes. The clergy soon realized the merits of this tuber and used their pulpits to spread the word, giving rise to the era of the potato preachers. Farmers were convinced, and a good thing too, because during the famine years from 1804 to 1814, potatoes were the mainstay of the Norwegian diet, a position the tuber has not relinquished.

The shopper can choose from a wide selection of Norwegian cheeses.

In the fall, the mountains are bursting with luscious berries, including blueberries, lingonberries (a tart, cranberrylike berry very popular in Norway and often made into jelly), and the less abundant cloudberries, a Scandinavian delicacy. In late summer, there are also bushes full of wild raspberries just waiting to be made into a scrumptious dessert.

CHEESE, ANYONE?

Norwegian cheeses include Gouda, Gudbrandsdal, Gamalost, Pultost, Jarlsberg, and Ridder, as well as goat cheeses and dessert cheeses. Gouda and Jarlsberg are the best known outside of Norway, and also the most popular in Norway. Gudbrandsdal is often called the most Norwegian cheese. First made in the 1850s in Fron in the Gudbrandsdalen area, this red cheese is most popular at the Norwegian breakfast table due to its sweet, caramelized flavor. Gamalost means old cheese, and this sharp-flavored cheese is well named, both for its pungent odor and because it has roots going back to Viking times.

DON'T SAY "CHOCOLATE," SAY "FREIA!"

From hot chocolate to candy bars, chocolate is a Norwegian passion. Every Norwegian consumes , on average, 17.6 pounds (8 kilograms) of chocolate a year. Half of this is produced by Freia.

Freia is Norway's most famous chocolate factory, immortalized in Norwegian-American Roald Dahl's enormously popular book, *Charlie and the Chocolate Factory*. Freia had its beginnings in 1892, when founder Johan Throne Holst, with his brother and brother-in-law, bought a small chocolate factory in the Rodelokka district in Oslo. From humble beginnings, Freia, which is still located in Rodelokka, is today one of Norway's success stories. One of every two chocolate bars sold in Norway is made by Freia, and Freia also exports chocolates all over the world.

Freia markets different varieties of chocolate bars: Firkløver, with almond flakes, is the snack bar for a mini pick-me-up during a busy day and KvikkLunsj, a chocolate-coated wafer, is the candy bar of choice for a hiking trip. Known outside Norway as "a little piece of Norway," Freia milk chocolate is smooth and rich.

Freia also gained the endorsement of famous Norwegian explorer Roald Amundsen, who stated after his return from his major South Pole expedition that Freia chocolate was one of his team's main sources of nourishment during the grueling journey.

Freia is a company with a social conscience. Promoting Norwegian culture and arts has become an inherent part of the company's mission. In 1920, Freia created the Freia Park, which is one of Oslo's finest parks, exhibiting the works of European sculptors, including Norwegian Gustav Vigeland. In 1922, Freia invited Norwegian artist Edvard Munch to decorate its employees' lunch room. And in 1934, Freia Hall, home to Oslo's Philharmonic Orchestra, was opened.

ARENDAL CAKES

3 eggs	³⁄₄ cup flour	2 tablespoons blanched
³⁄₄ cup sugar	¹⁄₄ teaspoon baking powder	almonds

Whisk two egg yolks and one whole egg with sugar until the mixture is light and creamy. Sift flour with baking powder and fold into the mixture.

Spoon dough onto a greased tin, and decorate with almond halves. Bake for 12 minutes in a moderate oven (170°C/325°F).

This recipe makes 40 Arendal cakes. (Arendal is in southern Norway.)

BEER AND WINE

Drinking beer is a Scandinavian tradition. During Viking times and the Middle Ages, beer was served at formal occasions. To make an agreement legally binding or to celebrate the baptism of an infant or a wedding, beer was served. As the price of beer is high in Norway, many Norwegians brew their own beer in the basements of their homes.

Wine is also a popular drink, but as Norway's climate is unsuitable for

Beer is particularly popular in the summer, and many restaurants do a roaring business in beer sales.

grape cultivation, Norwegians make wine from other fruits and from flowers. Wine-making is a popular hobby. Fruit and flower wines must be aged for a year, but, with their refreshing taste, are well worth the wait.

COFFEE

Traders brought coffee to Norway about 250 years ago, but as it was both foreign and expensive, only the wealthy consumed it. Modern Norwegians have made up for lost time with a vengeance. Today, Norwegians are among the world's biggest consumers of coffee per inhabitant. Norwegians are coffee purists and prefer to drink their coffee black to savor its full aroma and flavor. Guests are usually served coffee with cakes or *smørbrød*.

AQUAVIT—THE NATIONAL DRINK

Aquavit, Scandinavia's national drink and its contribution to the world's array of whiskeys, was first sold in the 16th century as a medicinal potion. Eske Bille, who created the drink in 1531, named it Aqua Vitæ, "a cure for all ills," and over the years this liquor graduated from medicinal potion to social beverage. Aquavit is made from potatoes and flavored with orange peel and several spices, including anise, fennel, caraway, and coriander.

The best-known aquavit in Europe is Linie Aquavit, or line aquavit, so called because the aquavit has passed over the equator. Many years ago, ships setting out from Trøndelag carried Norwegian aquavit on board as an export product. Not all the aquavit was sold, and when sampling the remainder, people noticed that the long journey had given the aquavit a new, enticing aroma. Since 1850, aquavit has been aged in oak vats on ships plying the route between Norway and Australia. Every bottle of aquavit has the name of the ship it was aged aboard, where it has been, and the duration of the journey recorded on its label.

Norwegians do not usually drink aquavit by itself but generally serve it to accompany a meal. It is usually served with a main course, in very small glasses, and is drunk at room temperature. The other side of the label on this bottle reads: "... this Aquavit has been carried on board Wilhelmsen's *M/S Tampa* around the world, crossing the Linie (equator) twice."

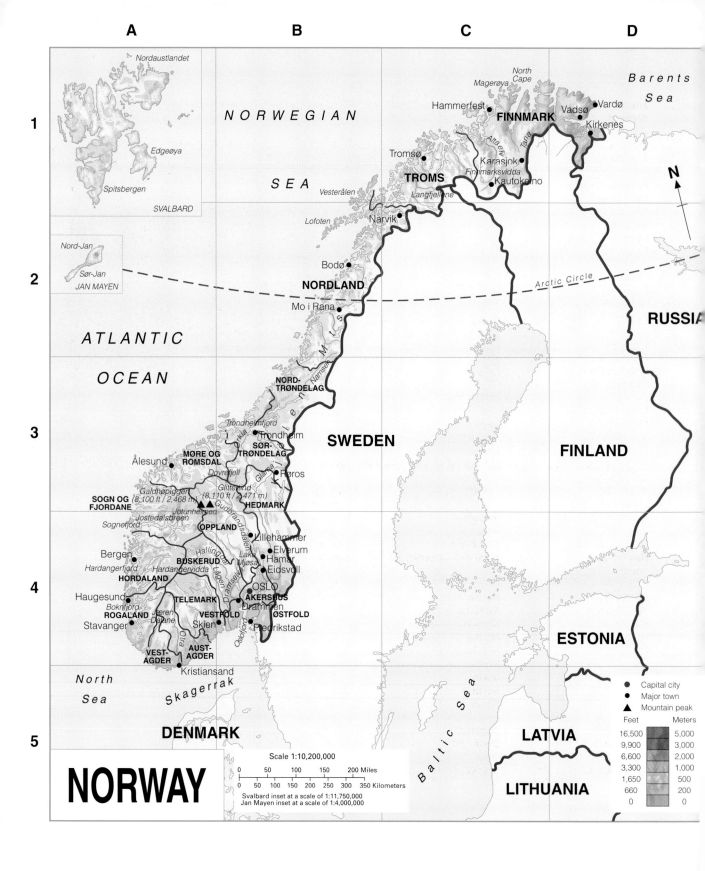

A **B** **C** **D**

Nordaustlandet

Edgeøya

Spitsbergen

SVALBARD

1

N O R W E G I A N

North
Cape

Magerøya

Hammerfest ●

FINNMARK

Vadsø ●
● Vardø

B a r e n t s
S e a

● Kirkenes

Nord-Jan

Sør-Jan

JAN MAYEN

S E A

Vesterålen

Tromsø ●

TROMS

Alta ev.

Karasjok ●

Finnmarksvidda

Tana

Kautokeino ●

Langfjellene

N

Lofoten

Narvik ●

2

A T L A N T I C

Bodø ●

NORDLAND

Arctic Circle

RUSSIA

O C E A N

Mo i Rana ●

SWEDEN

FINLAND

3

NORD-
TRØNDELAG

Trondheimfjord

Trondheim ●

SØR-
TRØNDELAG

Dovrefjell

Ålesund ●

MØRE OG
ROMSDAL

Glomma

Røros ●

Glittertind
(8,110 ft / 2,471 m)

SOGN OG
FJORDANE

Galdhøpiggen
(8,100 ft / 2,468 m)

Jotunheimen

▲ ▲

HEDMARK

Jostedalsbreen

Gudbrandsdalen

OPPLAND

Lillehammer ●

Sognefjord

Elverum ●

Bergen ●

BUSKERUD

Hallingdal

Lake
Mjøsa

Hamar ●
Eidsvoll ●

HORDALAND

Hardangerfjord

Hardangervidda

Lågen

Drammen

4

Haugesund ●

TELEMARK

OSLO ●

AKERSHUS

Drammen ●

ØSTFOLD

Boknfjord

ROGALAND

Jæren

Dalane

VESTFOLD

Skien ●

Oslofjord

Fredrikstad ●

Stavanger ●

Otra

VEST-
AGDER

AUST-
AGDER

● Kristiansand

ESTONIA

North
Sea

Skagerrak

B a l t i c   S e a

LATVIA

5

DENMARK

LITHUANIA

● Capital city
● Major town
▲ Mountain peak

Scale 1:10,200,000

0   50   100   150   200 Miles

0 50 100 150 200 250 300 350 Kilometers

Svalbard inset at a scale of 1:11,750,000
Jan Mayen inset at a scale of 1:4,000,000

Feet	Meters
16,500	5,000
9,900	3,000
6,600	2,000
3,300	1,000
1,650	500
660	200
0	0

NORWAY

QUICK NOTES

OFFICIAL NAME
Kongeriket Norge (in Norwegian), the Kingdom of Norway

AREA
Total area 164,283 sq. miles (387,266 sq. km.)
Mainland Norway, 125,017 sq. miles
(323,878 sq. km.)
Svalbard Islands, 39,000 sq. miles
(62,700 sq. km.)
Jan Mayen Island, 147 sq. miles (380 sq. km.)
Bouvet Island, 23 sq. miles (59 sq. km.)
Peter I Island, 96 sq. miles (249 sq. km.)
Dronning Maud Land

CAPITAL
Oslo

POPULATION
4.3 million

MAJOR LANGUAGES
Norwegian (Bokmål and Nynorsk)

MAJOR RELIGION
Church of Norway (Evangelical Lutheran)

GOVERNMENT
Hereditary constitutional monarchy with full parliamentary democracy

HEAD OF STATE
Executive power is formally vested in the monarch.

ROYAL FAMILY
Harald V, King of Norway (1937–), ascended the throne January 17, 1991, succeeding his father King Olav V.
Sonja, Queen of Norway (1937–)
Haakon, Crown Prince of Norway (1973–)
Martha Louise, Princess of Norway (1971–)

HEAD OF GOVERNMENT
Prime Minister

PARLIAMENT
The 165-seat Storting; elections are held every four years.

MAIN EXPORTS
Crude oil, natural gas, metals, pulp and paper, ships, machinery, fish and fish products, chemicals. Two-thirds of Norway's exports go to the European Union countries.

CURRENCY
Krone (NOK)
$1 = NOK7

LEADING ARTISTS
Edvard Grieg, composer (1843–1907)
Knut Hamsun, author (1859–1952)
Henrik Ibsen, playwright (1828–1906)
Edvard Munch, painter (1863–1944)
Arne Nordheim (1931–)
Sigrid Undset, author (1882–1949)
Gustav Vigeland, sculptor (1869–1943)
Henrik Wergeland, poet (1808–1845)

GLOSSARY

ætt ("eht")
Group of eight letters in the 24-rune alphabet.

barnehage ("BAR-neh-HAH-guh")
Kindergarten for children aged 4 to 7.

Bokmål ("BOOK-mawl")
Language developed during Norway's union with Denmark. The spoken form is different from Danish, but the written form is nearly identical to Danish.

bunad ("BOO-nahd")
Embroidered national dress.

fjord ("fyord")
Very deep and narrow inlet of the sea between steep cliffs.

futhark ("FEW-thark")
A name for the runic alphabet created by the first eight letters of the alphabet.

fylker ("FEWL-ker")
Counties; there are 19 counties in Norway, including the city of Oslo.

husmorlag ("HEWS-moor-lahg")
Neighborhood group of women who do projects of common interest, such as fundraising.

joik ("yoy-IK")
Sami musical tradition of yodeling that imitates animal sounds. *Joiks* include myths, Sami history, and commentaries on persons or current events.

Klar Melding ("klahr MEHL-ding")
"Clear message," a toll-free telephone hotline to the ombudsman for children to ask questions or present problems.

kommuner ("koo-MEW-ner")
Rural or urban district belonging to a county; each is administered by a council.

kvinnegruppe ("KVIN-nuh-GREW-puh")
Women's group formed to discuss women's issues and contemporary literature.

middag ("mid-DAHG")
Main meal of the day, eaten around 4–6 p.m.

Nynorsk ("NEE-noshk")
Language created in reaction to Danish rule, dating from the mid-1800s and combining elements from rural dialects for a more distinctly Norwegian language than Bokmål.

runes ("roons")
Angular letters of an ancient alphabet, one of the earliest forms of Germanic writing.

russ ("rewss")
High-school graduates celebrate their graduation wearing *russ* gowns. *Russ* describes both the gown and the graduate.

Samnorsk ("SAHM-noshk")
"Common Norwegian," a language created by 20th century language experts who sought to streamline Bokmål and Nynorsk into one language, to simplify communication between urban and rural areas and in the mass media.

Storting ("stoor-TING")
Norway's 165-member parliament.

vidder ("VI-der")
Mountain plateaus.

BIBLIOGRAPHY

Charbonneau, Claudette, and Patricia S. Lander. *The Land and People of Norway*. Harper Collins Children's Books, 1993.

Holte, Elisabeth. *Living in Norway*. New York: Abbeville Press, 1994.

Lerner Publications Co. *Norway in Pictures*. Minneapolis, MN: Lerner Publications, 1990.

Reynolds, Jan. *Far North: Vanishing Cultures*. San Diego: Harcourt Brace Jovanovich, Inc., 1992.

Vanbers, Bent. *Of Norwegian Ways*. New York: Barnes & Noble, 1992.

Zickgraf, Ralph. *Norway*. New York: Chelsea House, 1990.

INDEX

INDEX

INDEX

PICTURE CREDITS

Johan Berge: 8, 11, 12, 13, 16, 18, 20 (bottom), 21, 23, 63, 67, 70, 71, 84, 89, 90, 99, 102 (top and bottom), 110, 111, 118
Camera Press: 15, 36, 37, 38, 39, 42, 44, 59, 91, 92, 100, 104, 107
Focus Team: 1, 3, 4, 5, 6, 26, 57, 58, 60, 66, 115, 116, 120, 123
Hulton Deutsch: 28, 29, 32, 34, 35, 80, 93, 105
Hutchison: 65, 68, 83, 97
Image Bank: 14, 17, 19, 27, 46, 48, 50, 52, 53, 55, 75, 76, 114
International Photobank: 20 (top), 22, 30, 47, 49, 51, 54, 73, 74, 82, 88
Bjorn Klingwall: 40, 87
Life File: 7, 10, 103
Photobank: 56, 64, 72, 94, 96, 98, 108
David Simson: 81
Sonja Henie Center: 101
Elizabeth Su-Dale: 112, 113
Times Editions: 121